P9-CEP-425

FOREX REVOLUTION

In an increasingly competitive world, it is quality
of thinking that gives an edge—an idea that opens new
doors, a technique that solves a problem, or an insight
that simply helps make sense of it all.

We work with leading authors in the various arenas
of business and finance to bring cutting-edge thinking
and best-learning practices to a global market.

It is our goal to create world-class print publications
and electronic products that give readers
knowledge and understanding that can then be
applied, whether studying or at work.

To find out more about our business
products, you can visit us at www.ft-ph.com.

FOREX REVOLUTION

An Insider's Guide to the Real World of Foreign Exchange Trading

Peter Rosenstreich

Upper Saddle River, NJ • New York • London • San Francisco • Toronto
Sydney • Tokyo • Singapore • Hong Kong • Cape Town
Madrid • Paris • Milan • Munich • Amsterdam
www.ft-ph.com

Library of Congress Catalog Number: 2005921697

Publisher: Tim Moore
Executive Editor: Jim Boyd
Editorial Assistant: Kate E. Stephenson
Marketing Manager: Martin Litkowski
International Marketing Manager: Tim Galligan
Cover Designer: Alan Clements
Managing Editor: Gina Kanouse
Project Editor: Christy Hackerd
Copy Editor: Gayle Johnson
Indexer: Lisa Stumpf
Compositor: Tolman Creek Design
Manufacturing Buyer: Dan Uhrig

© 2005 by Pearson Education, Inc.
Publishing as Financial Times-Prentice Hall
Upper Saddle River, New Jersey 07458

Financial Times-Prentice Hall offers excellent discounts on this book when ordered in quantity for bulk purchases or special sales. For more information, please contact U.S. Corporate and Government Sales, 1-800-382-3419, corpsales@pearsontechgroup.com. For sales outside the U.S., please contact International Sales at international@pearsoned.com.

Company and product names mentioned herein are the trademarks or registered trademarks of their respective owners.

All rights reserved. No part of this book may be reproduced, in any form or by any means, without permission in writing from the publisher.

Printed in the United States of America

First Printing, June 2005

ISBN 0-13-148690-X

Pearson Education LTD.
Pearson Education Australia PTY, Limited.
Pearson Education Singapore, Pte. Ltd.
Pearson Education North Asia, Ltd.
Pearson Education Canada, Ltd.
Pearson Educatiòn de Mexico, S.A. de C.V.
Pearson Education—Japan
Pearson Education Malaysia, Pte. Ltd.

FINANCIAL TIMES PRENTICE HALL BOOKS

For more information, please go to www.ft-ph.com

Business and Society

John Gantz and Jack B. Rochester
> *Pirates of the Digital Millennium: How the Intellectual Property Wars Damage Our Personal Freedoms, Our Jobs, and the World Economy*

Douglas K. Smith
> *On Value and Values: Thinking Differently About We in an Age of Me*

Current Events

Alan Elsner
> *Gates of Injustice: The Crisis in America's Prisons*

John R. Talbott
> *Where America Went Wrong: And How to Regain Her Democratic Ideals*

Economics

David Dranove
> *What's Your Life Worth? Health Care Rationing…Who Lives? Who Dies? Who Decides?*

Entrepreneurship

Dr. Candida Brush, Dr. Nancy M. Carter, Dr. Elizabeth Gatewood, Dr. Patricia G. Greene, and Dr. Myra M. Hart
> *Clearing the Hurdles: Women Building High Growth Businesses*

Oren Fuerst and Uri Geiger
> *From Concept to Wall Street: A Complete Guide to Entrepreneurship and Venture Capital*

David Gladstone and Laura Gladstone
> *Venture Capital Handbook: An Entrepreneur's Guide to Raising Venture Capital, Revised and Updated*

Thomas K. McKnight
> *Will It Fly? How to Know if Your New Business Idea Has Wings… Before You Take the Leap*

Stephen Spinelli, Jr., Robert M. Rosenberg, and Sue Birley
> *Franchising: Pathway to Wealth Creation*

Executive Skills

Cyndi Maxey and Jill Bremer
> *It's Your Move: Dealing Yourself the Best Cards in Life and Work*

John Putzier
> *Weirdos in the Workplace*

Finance

Aswath Damodaran
> *The Dark Side of Valuation: Valuing Old Tech, New Tech, and New Economy Companies*

Kenneth R. Ferris and Barbara S. Pécherot Petitt
> *Valuation: Avoiding the Winner's Curse*

International Business and Globalization

John C. Edmunds
Brave New Wealthy World: Winning the Struggle for World Prosperity

Robert A. Isaak
The Globalization Gap: How the Rich Get Richer and the Poor Get Left Further Behind

Johny K. Johansson
In Your Face: How American Marketing Excess Fuels Anti-Americanism

Peter Marber
Money Changes Everything: How Global Prosperity Is Reshaping Our Needs, Values, and Lifestyles

Fernando Robles, Françoise Simon, and Jerry Haar
Winning Strategies for the New Latin Markets

Investments

Zvi Bodie and Michael J. Clowes
Worry-Free Investing: A Safe Approach to Achieving Your Lifetime Goals

Michael Covel
Trend Following: How Great Traders Make Millions in Up or Down Markets

Aswath Damodaran
Investment Fables: Exposing the Myths of "Can't Miss" Investment Strategies

Harry Domash
Fire Your Stock Analyst! Analyzing Stocks on Your Own

David Gladstone and Laura Gladstone
Venture Capital Investing: The Complete Handbook for Investing in Businesses for Outstanding Profits

D. Quinn Mills
Buy, Lie, and Sell High: How Investors Lost Out on Enron and the Internet Bubble

D. Quinn Mills
Wheel, Deal, and Steal: Deceptive Accounting, Deceitful CEOs, and Ineffective Reforms

Michael J. Panzner
The New Laws of the Stock Market Jungle: An Insider's Guide to Successful Investing in a Changing World

H. David Sherman, S. David Young, and Harris Collingwood
Profits You Can Trust: Spotting & Surviving Accounting Landmines

Michael Thomsett
Stock Profits: Getting to the Core—New Fundamentals for a New Age

Leadership

Jim Despain and Jane Bodman Converse
And Dignity for All: Unlocking Greatness through Values-Based Leadership

Marshall Goldsmith, Cathy Greenberg, Alastair Robertson, and Maya Hu-Chan
Global Leadership: The Next Generation

Management

Rob Austin and Lee Devin
Artful Making: What Managers Need to Know About How Artists Work

J. Stewart Black and Hal B. Gregersen
Leading Strategic Change: Breaking Through the Brain Barrier

Molly the love of my life.
And to Mom, Dad, Jon, and Rebecca the world's
most amazing family. Thanks for all the support.

Contents

4 The Basics of Foreign Exchange   45

10   What Moves the Markets: Basic Fundamental and Technical Trading Strategies   181

Preface

I love this market and it never stops amazing me. The foreign exchange market is the ultimate gauge of reality. In a world where it is impossible to quantify the actual significance of an event, the Forex market tries. In my view, just as in chaos theory, the Forex market is always moving from order into chaos and back to order again—and trading on the edge of chaos is the only place I want to be.

What makes foreign exchange trading existing are the underlying themes that drive the market. On the fundamental side, there are geopolitics, governments, societies, macroeconomics, and the behavior of the numerous market participants who vary greatly in objectives and approach. On the technical side, there is a market that seems to move in patterns and with endless liquidity. Life can become repetitive and slow, with some people even saying things like, "There is nothing new," or, "I've seen it all before." And I think, "Yeah, just you wait." As a Forex trader, you have a front-row seat to a world that never stops to amaze and produce the completely unexpected.

I wrote this book as an introduction to Forex trading in a simple and understandable format. It was not produced in response to some slick marketer screaming, "Make money in your sleep," or some academic with a mathematical model so complex that only four people in the world understand it. My intent is to provide a non-biased overview that will let the individual decide which approach to the market suits him or her best. With this knowledge, they can then choose their own advanced education and trading directions. I hope I can inspire aspiring Forex quants and instant traders alike.

To explain Forex trading, I use a blend of real trading experiences, definitions, and methodologies because you need all three to become a successful trader in any market. Trading is never about memorizing how someone else trades; one's strategy must be developed by the individual. Hopefully, with this book, you can take all of this information and begin crafting your own trading models. Good luck trading!

Acknowledgments

This book could not have been written without the input of some important people. Special thanks to the following people:

Vince and Jim Mezzetti and the rest of Myles Financial family

Brendon January—excellent research and analysis

Steve Nutland—Bank of America

James H. Sinclair and Nick Murray—Leslien-EBS Dealing Resources, Ergo-C

Drew Niv and Tim Koutroubas—FXCM

Pier Langone—an old friend and insightful trader

Barry Calder and Peter Burton—Hot Spot FX

Joachim Herr and Marc Hassinger—BMW

Gary Tilkin and Tim Gort—Global Forex Trading

Kathryn Page Camp and Sharon Pendleton—National Futures Association

Disclaimer

This book is sold with the understanding that neither the author nor the publisher is engaged in rendering legal, accounting, or other professional services or advice by publishing this book. Each individual situation is unique. Thus, if legal or financial advice or other expert assistance is required in a specific situation, the services of a competent professional should be sought to ensure that the situation has been evaluated carefully and appropriately. The author and the publisher disclaim any liability, loss or risk resulting, directly or indirectly, from the use or application of any of the contents of this book.

The opinions of any of the individuals mentioned in this book are their own opinions, and do not represent the opinions of the author, publisher or any other person or entity other than such individual.

1

THE TRULY MODERN MARKET

I love Asia: it smells of raw capitalism. Especially at night. Several years ago, I was watching Hong Kong in the evening as the city became a brilliant silhouette of pure commerce against the dark Communist backdrop of mainland China. The rickshaw drivers, rivers of neon lights, open-air markets, and steel high-rises always make me think of foreign exchange, the fundamental transaction of capitalism and the building block of modern globalization.

I couldn't speak Chinese, but as I approached a currency exchange booth on the Kowloon side of Hong Kong, I silently prepared to engage in an ancient conversation. I pulled out $100 in 20s, and the young man behind the counter smiled and said in broken

English, "I love LA, Hollywood. All right." He held his smile artificially long. "No," I said, "New York." "Ah," he replied, "Statue of Liberty. All right." And he smiled again. I was sure he could deliver a greeting in every language listed on the board behind him.

The electric board was black with red lights. It displayed the currency prices, a small flag for those who couldn't read the currencies, and a two-sided quote with a buy and sell price. The young man pulled out a beat-up calculator with masking tape holding down the screen and started to punch numbers. Exchange rate, buy side, times the number of U.S. dollars, 100, minus broker fee, equals 778 Hong Kong dollars. He looked up and I nodded in agreement. He unrolled a wad of colorful Hong Kong bills, counted them out carefully, and slid them over to me.

At that moment, it was hard to understand that in this little booth, lit by bad fluorescent lights, next to a vendor selling Peking duck and knock-off Chanel bags, I had access to the world's largest, most liquid, and most influential financial market—Forex.

A Market for the 21st Century

Since then, the Forex market has only grown more accessible, increased in size, and captured the public's attention. Spurred by investments in technology and communication over the past decade, the world is trading goods and services at ever-faster speeds, a process broadly called globalization. With the economic world drawing together faster, the Forex market has become its most critical market. And for the new breed of global trading and investors, the opportunities in Forex are just beginning (see Figure 1.1).

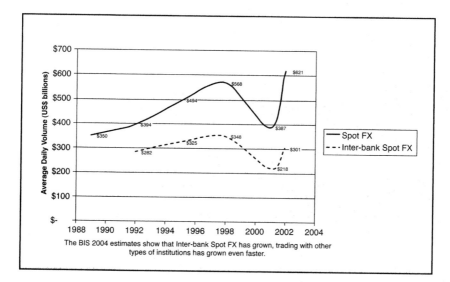

Figure 1.1—The increased popularity of retail Forex has assisted the sharp rise in trading volume.[1]

You can see globalization and trading today in cities around the world. Every morning at Grand Central Station in midtown Manhattan, tourists wait in line outside a well-lit and well-designed Travelers Money Exchange to trade their currency for dollars. With dollars in their pockets, they can dine out in Little India, buy cheap electronics in Chinatown, take a ride on the Staten Island Ferry, or do anything else money can buy.

This money fills up local cash registers, but it doesn't stay there for long. It is spent again. Perhaps it is used to buy some of the goods that are carried by ships into America's harbors. With their decks stacked impossibly high with containers, these ships steam past the Statue of Liberty and slide into docks bristling with giant cranes. The containers are whisked off the decks and hitched to tractor-trailers, which pull out onto the New Jersey Turnpike in an endless stream, carrying goods into the nation.

The goods are bought and the money flows back, much of it into New York again. Foreign corporations now look to trade the dollars they've made back into their native currencies. Far above the booths and lines of tourists, floors filled with brokers, traders, bankers, and trading terminals carry out these transactions.

Go to any major city in the world—New York, London, Tokyo, Bombay, Rio de Janeiro—and the same process is being carried out. This time, it may be British pounds or Japanese yen buying American goods and services, or foreign investors buying local stock or government securities. Billions of dollars flow back and forth across national borders every hour—sometimes passed by hand or voice, sometimes at the click of a button. At the end of each day, an average of $1.5 *trillion* has been traded, dwarfing the daily volume of the New York Stock Exchange, the NASDAQ, the FTSE, the DAX, and the Tokyo Nikkei combined.

It should come as little surprise that the volume is so high. Currencies bind the world together, form the bedrock of globalization, and are the means of exchange of world trade and investment.

But it isn't just the tourists and traders who participate in foreign exchange every day. So, most likely, do you. Take a typical day in the life of a Kansas resident. In the morning, he dresses in underwear made in China, a suit manufactured in Turkey, and a pair of shoes assembled in Italy. He brews a cup of coffee made of beans from Colombia. He drives a car with a transmission made in Japan and a steel frame from Canada. The gas powering the engine is refined from Saudi Arabian oil. At work, he turns on a computer fashioned with components made in Thailand, Indonesia, Taiwan, and China. The software is American.

All these goods were bought, and a portion of each purchase must be translated back into the currency of the country of origin. Although the Kansan may not be aware of it, his dollars are sent on a journey in which they are traded for yen, euros, baht, won, real, shekels, and yuan. We take this for granted, but without the currency market, our Kansan would be unable to get through the day unless his paychecks were issued in several currencies. Imagine trying to buy a hamburger in Kansas with yen! In short, foreign exchange has become woven into the fabric of our daily lives. It is impossible to be a resident of the modern world and avoid it.

After all, in these vast flows of money across borders lies an enormous investing opportunity. This market is old, but for the first time in history, due to a revolution in communication, technology, and credit, this market is available to small investors.

It's no coincidence that we are now seeing an enormous rise in Forex trading by both speculators and users. Forex is not a fad asset class pushed by analysts or created by an exchange to increase dwindling volume. It reflects fundamental market needs in today's environment.

A progressive market must meet two criteria today, and Forex has always met both. The market must be global, and it cannot be controlled by a single entity. The Forex market is truly global. It does not have a center and does not obey the rules of any one nation.

That applies especially to time. As different parts of the world move from darkness to light, trading activity comes to life. Currency is bought and sold in Tokyo while New York slumbers. When night descends on Tokyo, London offices are opening and starting to trade. By the time London approaches mid-afternoon, New Yorkers are arriving at their desks, ready to make money. The markets reflect these rhythms, with trading volume rising and falling depending on when workers are entering work or leaving to go home.

With this ability to trade the exact same currency at any time, the Forex can be called a 24-hour market that is open from late Sunday Eastern Standard Time, when the Forex week starts with the Monday morning open in Wellington, New Zealand, then on to Sydney,

Tokyo, Hong Kong, Singapore, Moscow, Frankfurt, London, and then finishing the week on Friday at five o'clock in New York (see Figure 1.2).

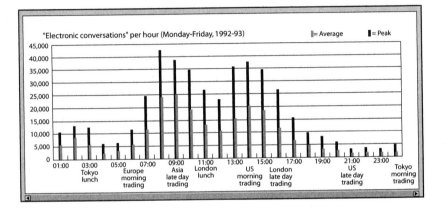

Figure 1.2—Daily trading activity of the foreign exchange market.

The Forex market also doesn't obey any one holiday schedule. New York banks don't close to celebrate May Day, but London does. London is open when Americans are sitting down to turkey dinners on Thanksgiving. Tokyo offices are filled on Christmas Day, when most Americans and Brits are at home unwrapping presents.

However, this vast market is united by two characteristics—ancient capitalism and new technology. At its core, the market is nothing new. The Forex market has roots that stretch back thousands of years, where cultures rubbed shoulders and merchants swapped goods at borders and in back alleys of ancient cities. This market grew out of itself—out of the human need to trade for goods that one society had but the other didn't. It grew out of the desire to make a profit.

For most of history, access was controlled by gatekeepers—merchants, bankers, industrialists—who wanted the profits for themselves. In the past 10 years, however, that has changed. Technology allows anyone with an Internet connection—via a terminal or cell phone—to not only trade Forex but also to have access to the information that gives traders a more level playing field.

Opportunity Is Knocking

Forex is an investing opportunity, one that can bring an investor profit or loss, provide a hedge for a portfolio, and be a source of critically important information—especially in a global investing environment where growth opportunities in the future will mostly be outside the U.S.

Forex is a volatile market intensified by leverage. Money is made (or lost) when investment values fluctuate. Although a market that moves up and down like a roller coaster can be nerve-wracking, it also offers more trading opportunities. Consider how the value of the dollar index changed between January 2002 and February 2004. The Australian dollar rose nearly 50 percent, the Euro almost 40 percent, the Swiss franc more than 30 percent, the British pound sterling 24 percent, the yen 22 percent, and the South Korean won more than 10 percent, according to *The Economist* (Feb. 9, 2004) (see Figure 1.3).

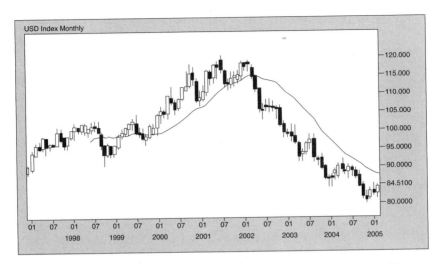

Figure 1.3—The Dollar Index is a weighted basket of G7 currencies used by traders to gauge relative strength.

Even if two currencies are not moving much against each other, investors can take advantage of small fluctuations through leverage. Compared to the wild tech days of the 1990s, trading a one-penny move wouldn't get anyone excited. But retail Forex is based on the power of leverage. This means that an investor can take a position with a small amount of money—say, $1,000—and leverage it into a position worth $100,000. This can be great when the markets move in a direction that benefits the original position, but losses pile up quickly when it does not.

An additional advantage of trading on Forex is that it offers investors invaluable education and experience—a "gateway" into the world of international investing. The oil shocks of the 1970s and the international economic crises of the 1990s taught many Americans that the U.S., even with its giant and diverse economy, depends as much on the global economy as the world depends on it. Combined with the weakening of the dollar's global dominance, high speculative returns from emerging markets, and the general sideways movement in the U.S. markets, savvy traders have expanded their search for investments. Any investor who does not have this perspective will miss opportunities. Taking part in the Forex market exposes an investor to the economic developments occurring around the world. With real money at stake, the investor will understand how political, social, and economic forces in other countries translate into profits or losses in the U.S. Thus, Forex offers not just portfolio exposure, but exposure for the investing mind. Over the next 50 years, most of the world's explosive economic growth is expected to take place outside the U.S. The Forex investor will be a part of it; the investor who stays home won't be. The new trading vernacular will be composed of terms such as bund, SET, and yuan.

Everybody's Talking About It

Another sign that the Forex market has come of age is that everyone's talking about it—investors, financial gurus, and world leaders.

Warren Buffet, whose Berkshire Hathaway fund has realized an average 22 percent increase in book value annually since 1965, announced in his 2003 letter to shareholders that he had, for the first time, entered the foreign exchange market on a large scale in 2002 and that he had increased his position in 2003.

Buffet attributed his move to the alarming increases in U.S. trade and government deficits. Buffet, one of the most successful investors in history, knows that weakness in the U.S. dollar could undermine the billions of dollars worth of assets he owns. "I feel more comfortable owning foreign-exchange contracts that are at least a partial offset to that position," he concluded.

In 2003, Morgan Stanley told its clients that they should take advantage of stock opportunities in Japan and Europe. The firm took that position because it believes stocks in those countries are undervalued and because it wants its clients to have a hedge against the further decline of the dollar. Stephen Roach, Morgan Stanley's chief economist in the U.S., warned that the dollar's value could not be sustained given the U.S. account and trade deficits. "America's massive current-account deficit cries out for a depreciation of the dollar," he wrote. (See http://www.globalagenda-magazine.com/2004/stephenroach.asp.)

The point here is not that investors should worry about the supposed imminent decline of the dollar (although a cautious, watchful eye would help), but that Wall Street believes investors should factor in currency fluctuations when planning their portfolios.

If the Forex market has drawn the attention of economists and market managers, political leaders have been incensed by it. Jacques Chirac, president of France, reportedly called aggressive foreign exchange traders the "AIDS of our economies."

Mahathir Mohamad, prime minister of Malaysia, blamed the economic troubles of the late 1990s in his country on "rogue speculators . . . anarchists wanting to destroy weak countries in their crusade for open societies, to force us to submit to the dictatorship of international manipulators." He openly called international financier George Soros a "moron."

Whether Forex is being touted by Wall Street or disparaged by politicians, there is little question that the market has arrived in the investing mainstream, and this role will only grow as globalization accelerates. As the world grows even closer together over the next two decades, the question every investor should ask himself is how he should handle the change.

Endnotes

1. Source: EBS.

2

THE CURRENCY OF TRADING IN EVERYDAY LIFE

A Fact of Life

It is essential to understand that Forex is a market that plays out in everyday life in a way that other markets do not. A fluctuation in currency value can have an impact on a nation's social, political, and economic conditions. In extreme situations, a nation's entire political structure can be shaken to the core.

Because of these high stakes, a government often uses all its power to control the value of its currency. It may decide that to protect its private citizens from international traders and stabilize its economy the government needs to control how its currency is traded. China, for example, has "pegged" its currency to the U.S. dollar, meaning that it has set a tight conversion rate of $1 to 7.27 yuan.

This peg has defied market forces, which are pushing for the yuan to float against the dollar because of the huge trade imbalance between the two countries. But China has kept the peg, worried that simply allowing its currency to appreciate against the dollar would damage its economic growth and possibly throw its tightly monitored society into turmoil.

Japan also exercises strong control over its currency, unlike its developed counterparts, the U.S. and Europe, which allow their currencies to float more freely. At its basic level, Japan is an export-driven economy that understands currency fluctuations. Exports powered Japan Inc. through the '70s and '80s. There are two ways for an export country to stay competitive: be innovative or be cheaper than the competition.

Japan had been both, and it ruthlessly grabbed market share and put American competitors out of business. In the early '90s, however, that began to change. The yen rose in value, and even cheaper and nimbler competitors appeared in Southeast Asia. Suddenly, Japan Inc. began to lose its luster. Japanese companies, like their American competitors a decade before, were forced to send work overseas, and unemployment mounted. Japan, however, had a tightly knit society that could not sustain these shocks. The country has since decided not to allow its currency to rise too sharply. In 2003 alone, the country intervened in markets eight times to manage its currency fluctuations. It bought billions of U.S. dollars and sold the yen, thereby helping control the value of the U.S. dollar/yen trade.

Traders must realize that when they take a position on the Japanese yen—or any other country's currency, for that matter— they are dealing with a government that sees the value of its currency as an essential tool to protect its economic and social stability. Even a Forex trader who uses purely technicals to trade must beware of these unique factors and of the broader lesson that currencies are not just another investment to be traded.

If a stock plunges one day, it may be damaging to some investors. If it's a bellwether stock, such as Intel, it might lead to a market sell-off that hits a lot of investors in the wallet. Eventually, this might play out by signaling that the economy is slowing down, with all the accompanying pains that such a slowdown brings. But unless a stock market crashes in dramatic fashion, people continue to live their lives, mostly oblivious to or uncaring whether the market is up or down from day to day.

Fluctuations in the Forex market, however, can have an immediate effect on people throughout society, no matter how rich or how poor. A change in the foreign exchange rate can mean that middle-class luxuries such as cars and houses are suddenly too expensive. A more severe change can make it difficult to feed one's family.

Keeping Up with the Rates

Because of its tremendous power in local life, currency rates are regularly monitored all over the world. Outside the U.S., people watch exchange rates like Americans follow the Dow. In Sri Lanka, taxi drivers can reel off exchange rates as well as New York's foreign exchange desk dealers.

Americans may soon have to as well. As the world becomes more interconnected, the traditional stability Americans have enjoyed from their currency may be eroded. The newly introduced euro might ultimately supersede the U.S. dollar. Many nations rely on the U.S. dollar as a reserve currency, which helps sustain its value. If nations start using the euro for this role, the U.S. dollar could be exposed to unprecedented fluctuation. In the fall of 2004, with the U.S. Congress issuing $800 billion in new debt, the market began to question the U.S.'s "risk-free" status, opening the window for other currencies to fill this void.

The Sun Never Sets on Forex

I learned these lessons long before I began to trade currencies myself. They were the result of my travels, when I saw firsthand the role of currencies and their potential for trading. One of the strongest impressions I received was in Thailand in 1999.

Noodles in the Morning

It was very clear that something devastating had happened. I was sitting in a restaurant in Bangkok, Thailand, enjoying a lunch of noodles and gazing at the city skyline. It looked as if it had been ravaged by a plague or war. Towers stood half-built, dark and empty. Cranes were motionless steel skeletons.

Two years before, Bangkok's skyline was swarming with workers and alive with movement. The Thai economy was growing at torrid rates, and the land was awash with money. Visitors saw scenes of jarring contrasts in the streets of Bangkok, where an ancient culture had entered the modern era at warp speed.

The rich steered sleek Mercedes past street cleaners riding elephants and peasants tugging water buffaloes to market. Shopping malls, shiny with goods, attracted people from the countryside to gawk and marvel. Some could not grasp the concept of private property upon which the new prosperity had been built. They roasted fish over open fires on the mall's marble floors until they were shooed away by security guards.

Even the seasonal rhythms of nature were blunted and tamed. In 1997, Bangkok authorities used engineering to divert the brackish waters that flooded the streets every year during the monsoon season—for the first time in the city's history.

Thailand was riding high atop a financial revolution brought about by a nexus of Internet technology, investing tools, and new attitudes. The Internet had freed the enormous pools of capital in New York, Tokyo, and London. The money burst free, pouring through high-speed fiber-optic cables into the country, where it swelled lines of credit and financed new golf courses, office complexes, and ambitious municipal projects. A German firm was contracted to build a sky train between Bangkok's downtown and the suburban malls.

Then, abruptly, the boom turned to bust. Creditors grew concerned that the lavish projects were actually money pits and boondoggles. The Thai economy couldn't produce enough goods to balance the funds coming into the country, and the currency wobbled under the pressure. Investors were spooked. Just as it had arrived, the money vanished back through the fiber cables, and the financial house of cards it had supported collapsed.

I could still see the effects two years later as I slurped my meal. Banks failed, credit dried up, and workers walked off multimillion-dollar construction projects, leaving their tools scattered. There was no money to pay them. The sky tram was almost finished, but one ride was rumored to cost half a day's salary. It rode back and forth, empty, to malls where no one could afford to shop.

History has many examples of financial catastrophes, but few with the force and speed of the one that hit Thailand. Prosperity had shot the Thai society centuries forward into the modern era and then torn it up by its roots. Laid-off workers, facing unprecedented inflation and lost savings, filled the streets, rocking a stable government.

The power of foreign exchange to build and destroy struck me. Of course, other markets today create and vaporize wealth all the time. But those losses seemed trivial compared to how the foreign exchange market had devastated Thailand.

The Forex market, however, affects everyone, from the street cleaner to the executive in his palatial suite atop a new office building. It could literally make and then break a social order.

Laos for Lunch

Thailand taught me the destructive power of the currency markets, but it was in neighboring Laos that I learned it was also an excellent trading vehicle.

I was still in Thailand when my friend and I planned a trip to Laos. While she studied the *Let's Go* guide, I scanned the currency prices in the *Bangkok Record* and on lighted boards outside exchange vendors. The aftershocks of the Southeastern currency crisis could still be felt in Laos. The economy was weak at best. The country's currency—the kip—was directly linked to and reliant on Thailand and foreign investment for survival, which didn't bring more stability. In fact, at the borders of Laos and Thailand the agents would accept only U.S. dollars or baht for entry fees, rejecting their own unstable kip.

As I crossed over the border into Laos in February 2000, one U.S. dollar bought 7,500 kip, one Thai baht bought 200 kip, and 37 Thai baht bought one U.S. dollar. I was a poor student in Southeast Asia, desperate to shave off any cost of living that I could. The currency exchange rate seemed like the ideal way.

Because of the exchange rate mechanism, all currencies are in balance (efficient markets with no opportunity to arbitrage). But there was a very viable gray market. Each participant in this market needed or valued a specific currency differently. The banks wanted U.S. dollars for stability, and the street vendors preferred baht because it was safe and convenient. The kip was good for small purchases such as noodles.

The nice thing about physically trading a currency such as the kip was its large exchange rate denominations. Each time I traded dollars for kip, I could easily make a 1,000- or 2,000-kip profit. I know that isn't much more than a few pennies, but that wasn't the point. The point was that I could count the returns. After a few transactions I was up 10,000 kip, and that was literally a stack of cash I had generated from nothing.

Armed with the buy/sell exchange rates, I toured Laos—a living, breathing trading desk. Each day, I looked for banks, money exchangers, or private individuals who would offer exchange prices better than my base price.

At first I was looking for straight cash exchanges. A participant would say he would give me 210 kip for one baht. Because I knew the bank exchange rate was 200, I would make a few kip. Other times I would find arbitrage in the exchange of goods and services. A cab ride was 40 baht or $1; I could pick the better trade.

I was hooked. I spent my whole trip looking for exchange rates. And the kip started to build up. After a few days, I had made enough to buy a lunch of noodles and a French-style sandwich on my profits in the streets of Laos's capital, Vientiane.

Odessa at Dusk

In 1994, I was in Odessa, Ukraine, basically touring under the guise of studying world history for my BA. Odessa was in a unique state of flux caused by severe economic crisis. The Soviet Union had collapsed just a few years before, allowing the smaller states around Russia to spin off into independent countries. Odessa was now a part of the independent nation of Ukraine.

As in many newly formed nations, the economic situation was volatile. Between 1992 and 1996, the karbovanet, the Ukrainian currency, was ravaged by hyperinflation and fluctuation. In 1992, one dollar could buy 208 karbovanet. In 1995, that same dollar was worth 147,463 karbovanet.

The wild fluctuations created a few interesting situations for me and my fellow travelers. First was the sheer size of the number of bills created by a simple exchange of $20. It was like winning the jackpot at a casino. I walked out of there with all my pockets bulging. You'd get a block of currency 6 inches square.

Second, and more important, was the constantly changing exchange rate. Between breakfast and dinner, the value of the money in my pocket could easily drop 20%. Imagine having a $10 bill in the morning that was worth $8 when you spent it in the evening. In addition, the largest swings occurred when Odessa was sleeping and traders in New York and Asia caused the currency's value to move around. Ukrainians would wake up and find that the value of the karbovanet was half of what it was when they went to sleep.

To avoid these pitfalls, I exchanged only the amount of money I could spend in a single day. The karbovanet was weakening any-way, so there was a greater chance of the U.S. dollars in my pocket gaining strength over time. This strategy was helped by the fact that there was nothing really to buy in Odessa except used Russian military gear and vodka.

But for other people, the solution was not so simple. I had the benefit of having my net worth in U.S. dollars. But what if I were a Ukrainian, and my worth was in karbovanets? In this case, my eco-nomic fate was in the hands of traders halfway around the world.

Late one afternoon on a weekday, I went to a small newsstand to pick up a pack of cigarettes. The owner almost knocked me over in his haste to close up shop. I said all I wanted was a pack of cigs, making a motion that I would be quick. He eyed me suspiciously for a second and grunted OK. He let me in the store, and I made the purchase.

I carefully asked him what the rush was, and he responded that he needed to go exchange his cash for the day. He said if he didn't hurry, the exchange would close, and holding Ukrainian money overnight was too risky. We finished our transaction and he moved swiftly out the front, locked the door, and was gone down one of Odessa's old streets.

Back in a 9-to-5 Market

These experiences were far different from the lessons I learned growing up.

My father's attitude toward investing was conservative. He always said to buy blue chips—buy them and hold them. In the long run, he told me, that's how you make consistent returns.

So when I looked to start a career in finance, I didn't stray outside the realm of traditional investing. I took an internship at a major firm in Greenwich, Conn. This was my entrée onto Wall Street.

But even before I started, my perspective had begun to change. I have always had a contrarian streak, and I had traveled abroad and read much about the history of other cultures. Increasingly, I began to doubt the prevailing wisdom that a patient investor is rewarded over time.

To me, even as the world grew closer, it had also become increasingly unstable and volatile. The speed of change had become so great that it often was chaotic. Just think of the whole dot-com explosion. From this perspective, entering into a long-term investment strategy seemed risky. My investments were sitting ducks, exposed to market risk for extended amounts of time. Perhaps, I thought, times had changed, and a new investing perspective and corresponding strategy were needed.

So I put on my best suit and headed to my new Greenwich office. What I found was pretty much what I expected. I was working under a broker and his assistant, who put me in a cubicle watching tech stocks on a computer screen—Compaq, to be exact. They really didn't know how to handle the new volatility inherent in these speculative issues. So I spent a lot of my days just watching the markets.

Watching these blinking numbers for hours, day after day, I realized that the world and the equity markets had changed but the brokers had not. They were still investing their clients' money like it was 1950. Their philosophy continued to be buy and hold, and believe that in the end, time would heal all investment wounds.

But this no longer worked. Although the market indexes—the Dow and the S&P 500—still showed strong returns, the individual companies on these indexes had become much more risky than the blue chips of the past. Think about it—few of the top 50 American companies from the '70s, '60s, or '50s have survived to the present day. So why should an investor believe that the companies listed today will be there in 10 or 20 years?

My boss in Greenwich had been in the business for decades and wasn't going to change. He would advise his clients to buy "good solid companies" and hold them, whatever happened.

Before I go any further, let me say clearly that I still believe a diversified buy-and-hold strategy is suitable for the core portion of any investor's portfolio, but another part of the portfolio needs to be flexible, opportunistic, and aggressive. Not in the sense of taking extravagant risk, but having a philosophy of rapid action and defense. Practitioners would call this dynamic allocation.

(At another asset management firm I worked at, the directors said they could do nothing to protect their clients after the stock market bubble burst in 2001. They just watched as the market took back five years of gains and more. I'm confident the same thing happened at my old firm in Greenwich.)

So there I sat in Greenwich, watching a single stock that my boss didn't understand. After a while, I began to think that his investment strategy wasn't "buy and hold" but "hold and pray."

If the market spiked or plunged, he wouldn't exit. If the market environment changed, he wouldn't take a defensive position or create a new strategy. Perhaps he had a little concern, but no real plan of action.

Another strong impression was the lack of connection that stock speculation had with the real world. As soon as a stock begins to trade in the secondary market, the gains or losses affect primarily the speculators in the stock. Even the company isn't directly affected. If a solid company's stock drops from $100 to $1, this doesn't change daily business or the lifestyle of individuals (unless they were hoping to cash out).

These experiences had a profound effect on me. They steered me toward the Forex market, gave me an understanding of the currency markets, and helped me develop trading strategies.

Many traders, entering the Forex market for the first time, have been led to believe that it is just like any other market, and that their skill sets are easily interchangeable. That is only partly correct. Without a broader understanding of the role Forex plays in the world, a trader will realize lower returns and may even fail to reap a profit.

And that is the basis of my approach to the Forex market. The best traders don't see the market as just prices moving up and down, regardless of actual trading style, but as a fundamental part of a society and the world economy.

3

THE HISTORY OF FOREX (AND WHY YOU SHOULD CARE)

The Beautiful Market

Foreign exchange today may seem too complex for the average person to grasp. The images of the market that dominate the media—walls of blinking computer screens, screaming traders, giant blocks of money traded at the speed of light, defined by an intricate interplay of events—reinforce this perception. But these images are actually part of a façade, masking a relatively simple transaction.

At its heart, each foreign exchange is a trade—an exchange of one monetary unit (currency) for another. Dealers and investors may employ intricate strategies or use technical trading language and develop rich models, but that doesn't fundamentally alter the act.

Understanding this helps cut through the clutter, misperceptions, and mystery that surround this market. Very little of what is done in foreign exchange today is vastly different from how individuals have traded for thousands of years. The techniques and tools have changed, but the simple exchange remains the same.

Because foreign exchange is in fact so old, it is important to trace its roots, to explore how this market has evolved over the millennia. Individuals—kings and emperors, traders and dealers, common citizens and thieves—have employed all kinds of methods to use money and markets to their advantage. Their strategies have resulted in success and disaster. But all contain examples and lessons that will be helpful for the modern investor to understand this market.

This chapter also looks at the nature of money, how it has been used by different societies throughout history, and how its value can fluctuate. What emerges is the story of a long struggle between government and markets over who gets to control money—a struggle that continues to this day.

Lessons of History

One of the most famous and vivid channels of foreign exchange occurred along the fabled "Silk Road"—over which goods flowed back and forth between Asia, the Middle East, and Europe. The road started in Xian, a city in central China, and went by various trails west. Centuries ago, traders prodded columns of camels loaded with rugs, silks, and bags of aromatic spices that Europeans needed to season their dishes and delight their palates. Through the city's alleys and in its open market spaces, goods were inspected, values suggested, and deals struck. Money and objects changed hands.

This kind of trade is the barter system, which is still the norm in many parts of the world. However, the barter system had flaws. For one, making individual trades was cumbersome and time-consuming. Each item had to be inspected and its worth determined before haggling could even begin.

Two, it was inefficient. Goods didn't always match up in value, so bartering required an extensive number of items to make the trade even. A bag of grain may not be exactly worth a lamb, so the trader would have to add a bottle of wine to even things out. This made things much more complex.

Three, the barter system could leave out vast parts of society. What happens if the farmer wants meat but doesn't need a pair of shoes? The farmer trades his grain with the butcher. But the shoemaker, who needs grain as much as the butcher, is left out.

There is a solution to the problems of the barter system, and many cultures developed it—currency.

The Roots of Modern Currency

Forget the idea that currency is a piece of colored paper with a picture of someone famous on it. Paper money as it now exists is a relatively new concept, and it probably won't survive our lifetimes. In cultural and historical terms, currency is something that any group mutually recognizes as valuable.

For example, the Aztecs prized cacao beans, which were used to make a delicious chocolate drink. Part of the beans' value derived from the fact that they were also practical. They could be transported relatively easily, were uniform, and made bartering simpler. If a trade was uneven, a merchant could throw in a scoop or two of beans.

The ancient Romans valued salt, an essential spice to liven up dishes and replenish the body during hot Mediterranean summers. Like the Aztec cacao beans, salt was also practical. It could be cut into small, uniform units and was accepted everywhere. Roman soldiers, who sweated during maneuvers under their leather and armor, were paid in salt. The Latin word for salt, *sal*, is the root of *salary*.

In North America, we still refer to one dollar as a *buck*—few understanding that *buck* once referred to deerskin, which was commonly used as an item of exchange in colonial times.

Everywhere, currency was determined by local conditions. East Asians often used rice, Mongolians used bricks of tea, and Native Americans in the Northeast used colored shells.

The introduction of currency marked an important advance in a society's economic life. Instead of simply trading items, people could determine value through something universal. Currency allowed exchanges to be more circular, rather than a chain of one-on-one transactions. The shoemaker could now sell his wares to the butcher for currency and then use that currency to buy the grain he needed.

Value, of course, is a relative term, and cultures often found that what they treasured did not inspire the same reverence in their neighbors. One tribe in Alaska used dog teeth as currency, something other tribes regarded as disgusting. The aristocrats of Yap, an island in the South Pacific, used giant sandstone slabs so large that they needed dozens of laborers to move them. For obvious reasons, this currency never gained wide use.

As ancient cultures grew more sophisticated and trade grew to unprecedented levels, they found themselves back in the same barter system as before, with all its faults. The problem was to find something that was recognized as valuable, even among different cultures with different languages and beliefs.

The solution to this problem appeared in 640 BC in a civilization on the coast of what is today Turkey. This invention would establish the first international currency and lay the groundwork for our modern economic system—the metal coin.

The small kingdom of Lydia had grown rich through its production of high-quality cosmetics and perfumes, which it sold to other lands throughout the eastern Mediterranean.

The Lydians were the first, it appears, to mint coins. Metal, of course, had long been recognized as a valuable substance by many cultures. Gold, with its alluring luster, its malleable quality, and the fact that it never rotted or rusted, was held in high esteem. As early as 2500 BC, Mesopotamian clay tablets carried inscriptions that recorded the use of silver and gold as payments. But these payments were usually in large quantities. Gold was too scarce and valuable to be used in small exchanges.

This changed when the Lydians began stamping the first coins, which were about the same size as a modern quarter but much thicker. Several could be easily carried around in a bag. These first coins were made from a naturally occurring mixture of gold and silver called electrum. To make sure everyone, including illiterate farmers, could determine the value of the coins, the Lydians stamped them with a lion's head.

It is difficult to overestimate the impact these coins made as they began to circulate among the empires that ringed the Mediterranean Sea. Uniform coins meant merchants did not have to use scales to measure metal, a time-consuming process. A glance could determine literally how much money was on the table. Even in 600 BC, traders knew the importance of time and convenience.

Lydia produced more coins, with newer versions fashioned of solid gold. Money begot money. Attracted by the standard coins, merchants began setting up their goods in a central spot where people could browse among different stalls for goods—dishes, beer, olive oil, cloth. The market, not unlike the modern shopping mall, was born.

Although the Lydian empire soon crumbled, its innovation in using coins spread through the Mediterranean world. This was the first international economic system as we would understand it.

It is here that we can first see the revolutionary impact that money has had on society. Most ancient groups were small and organized around the principle of kinship. Going outside that society, because of fears, xenophobia, and misunderstandings, was rare. Most transactions involved one person speaking to another.

The value of money in the form of coins, however, was recognized between cultures. You did not need to speak the same language or have the same cultural background. Thus, societies could easily join and create an economy far more complex, diverse, and large than anything seen before.

In the late fourth century BC, Alexander the Great led his armies to victory through central Asia and into India. Alexander's empire was, for the first time in history, a commercial empire. Alexander did not just demand tribute from the conquered peoples. He yoked them into a new economic order by building cities with open markets in their center. Merchants quickly moved in, using the trusted Greek coins as a medium of exchange. The Greek language, in a heavily accented, simplified form, was used by merchants of different cultures to haggle and exchange goods.[1]

These characteristics are not too dissimilar from the world today, where international business is largely based on the dollar and deals made after a discussion in pigeon English. Alexander's period could be called the first era of globalization. Our modern era, with its markets and means of exchange, is not fundamentally different.

The Clash Between Governments and Markets

As the use of currency spread, governments began taking steps to exert their control over it. This should hardly be surprising. Whoever controls currency holds power, and governments almost always seek power.

For thousands of years, Chinese emperors relied on a bureaucracy and a powerful army to control the use of money in their kingdom. As far back as 500 BC, tokens made from copper or brass were issued and circulated as cash. These tokens, which were strung together on strings, were backed up by gold and silver held by the government. Private citizens were forbidden to possess these metals on their own. No one could refuse the tokens, and the state maintained absolute control over the monetary supply and its value. This system is quite different from the metal coins issued by the Lydians, which had intrinsic value and were difficult for any state to keep track of once they had entered circulation.

The tokens were eventually replaced by two products of Chinese ingenuity—paper and printing. Sometime in the first millennium, paper made from mulberry tree bark was stamped with the Chinese emperor's seal and backed up with gold. These bills, often the size of a modern sheet of notebook paper, were far easier to transport and use than the strings of bulky tokens. They are some of the first examples of paper money in history.

In the 1200s, most of China fell under the control of Mongolian emperors, whose vast horse armies would conquer much of Asia and terrorize populations as far away as Poland and the Middle East. The Mongolian emperors understood instinctively that loose money was a threat to their power.

Like the previous emperors, the Mongols issued paper money and forbade private citizens from holding any gold and silver on their own. Anyone who did not accept these bills was severely punished. Another threat were foreign traders, who could theoretically bring money into the empire and thus upset the state's monopoly.

Elaborate precautions were taken to ensure that this did not happen. Merchants entering China had to surrender all their money to a government official, who then paid the merchants' expenses with the emperor's paper money. Foreigners were kept under strict watch while in the empire. Sketches were made of them at the border for quick identification. Merchants had to report to the police whenever they stopped for the night and had to submit to searches each evening and morning.

The Chinese system of paper money held together as long as the emperor's power was absolute. But no government system survives forever. In the late 1300s, the Chinese Emperor Ming decided to pay the 100,000 artisans who lived in the Forbidden City and its 60,000 guards in paper money. Whenever more money was needed, more money was printed. Marco Polo was stunned to observe the emperor's bureaucrats stamping these slips of paper, which the Chinese used faithfully to exchange for real goods. But the faith was soon lost as the market was flooded with paper. By 1420, the emperor's paper money brought only 1/40 of its original value.

This story illustrates another trait of currency—its value fluctuates. Much of this depends on the laws of supply and demand. If a currency is too scarce—say, diamonds—there will not be enough of it to use in everyday transactions, and the economy will be strangled. But if a currency is too common, its value will plunge. If gold existed in great quantities in any streambed, for example, it would have no value.

Great influxes of gold have wrought great change to prices. When Spaniards in the 1500s brought back shiploads of gold from the Americas, the surge in gold ignited inflation and launched a price revolution.

This was unintentional. Most Spaniards were unaware of the economic relationship between an increase in the money supply and an increase in prices. But other leaders soon learned something that modern governments seem to understand intuitively—if you need more money, simply make more of it.

In the fifteenth and sixteenth centuries, both French and English kings found themselves heavily in debt. One, the dauphin in France, used his control over mints to melt down silver and reissue it as coins—mixed with a base alloy. Far more coins were dumped into the local economy, and the dauphin was able to pay his debts. Inevitably, however, inflation soon set in, and in Paris the coins were no longer trusted as a form of currency.[2]

In England, Henry VIII tried a similar tactic. He hoarded silver and then announced that new silver coins would be revalued higher, even as he added an alloy to make more of them. In the short run, the tactic worked, and Henry eventually took so much silver out of coins that they had to be coated to display a metallic sheen. Henry VIII is rightly remembered in history for many things. To economic historians, he is the author of "the Great Debasement."

Both Henry and the dauphin profited enormously from their debasement schemes, but the effect on common people—especially the poor—was destructive. The debased coins ignited inflation, raising the prices of everything from bread to livestock. The poor fell further and further into debt and were dispossessed of goods and homes. In England, the peasants revolted. Unrest, hardship, and war were the products of abusive monarchs.

These abuses generated a backlash, especially against the power monarchies had to manipulate the currency for their short-term goals. The English philosopher John Locke, champion of reason and the Enlightenment, made a novel proposal. He suggested that money was of a set value and that the value should be honored—regardless of what the country's rulers thought or desired. This was a radical idea, and one that the royalty did not appreciate. The king held the power of the purse, but this reform would effectively sew the purse shut. The market, not the king, would determine a currency's value, and the market had to be respected and its rules obeyed, or the people would suffer.

Understanding the long struggle between government and the market is critical to understanding the Forex market today. Although kings and queens no longer rule over their subjects and the treasury as they once did, governments still spend money voraciously. When deficits balloon and credit is ruined, they often resort to tricks rather than making the painful and necessary decision to rein in their appetites, raise taxes, or both.[3]

This is where the market comes in. Because money today holds no intrinsic value—it's simply an article of faith (our word *credit* comes from the Latin *credere*, to believe or put faith in)—someone must ensure that it is worth as much as a nation says it is. Forex investors, from the smallest to the largest, exercise the will of the market. It can be ruthless and sometimes scary, but it is also vitally necessary. Money is far too important to be controlled by government.

Of course, governments don't like to be told how to run their affairs, and they'll do virtually anything to retain control. In each case, however, the market is never wholly defeated. Black markets and underground trading schemes always grow up outside government control, no matter how earnest or effective police surveillance is. The market is always seeking true value, a spot where it can reach equilibrium.

This battle between markets and government is never-ending. A currency is often regarded with patriotism and pride, not to mention as a symbol of legitimacy for the government. If a currency appears wobbly or devalues, so do a nation's leaders. This is why governments often openly detest currency speculators as ruthless parasites who cause and then profit from disorder.

It will never be safe to say that the market, or the governments, have truly won. The influence of Forex has caused a backlash. In 1978, Nobel Prize-winning economist Jame Tobin proposed that major economies levy a uniform tax on all foreign exchange transactions. The idea was called the "Tobin tax." Tobin said a small tax would allow currencies to be traded but would discourage currency speculators from shifting currency around the world simply to take advantage of tiny differences in value. Naturally, politicians, especially those who dislike the free market anyway, have taken up Tobin's idea. They say that speculators have little respect or regard for nations or cultures. As we have already noted, currency fluctuations can devastate a society and ruin budgets. The Tobin tax, if it is enacted, could be fairly described as governments' revenge.

In its defense, conservatives point out that the private market is a critically important check on government power. Market discipline keeps the government from dominating a society. In the most idealistic terms, Forex investors around the world are in a constant struggle to keep governments honest.

Trends That Rocked the Forex World

The Rise and Fall of the Modern Gold Standard

The horror and destruction of two world wars filled the minds of the men who gathered in 1944 in Bretton Woods, Vt. They were determined to set the world right again and lay the foundation for a new international economic order. The core of this system was the strict pegging of all western currencies—British pounds, French francs, German marks—to the U.S. dollar. The U.S. dollar in turn was based on a set amount of gold—hence, the modern gold standard.

The Bretton Woods system, however, was fated to ultimately collapse. The reason became starkly clear over time. Banks needed the U.S. dollar, which was pegged to gold, to establish security in their reserve banks. The central banks of Europe could not circulate more money in their own economies if that meant overrunning the number of dollars they held. This system depended, then, on the U.S. running dollar deficits with the rest of the world, and the number of dollars in circulation soon exceeded the amount of gold backing them up.

With more and more dollars in circulation, it became clear that the U.S.'s pledge to back up its paper money in gold was more and more hollow. By the early 1960s, an ounce of gold could be exchanged for $40 in London, even though the price in the U.S. was $35. This difference showed that investors knew the dollar was overvalued and that time was running out.

Investors were not the only ones to recognize the fundamental imbalance of the Bretton Woods system. American economist Robert Trifflin had first identified the problem in 1960—for which he has since been honored by having it named "Trifflin's Dilemma."

There was a solution to Trifflin's Dilemma for the U.S.—reduce the number of dollars in circulation by cutting the deficit and raise interest rates to attract dollars back into the country. Both these tactics, however, would drag the U.S. economy into recession, a prospect new President John F. Kennedy found intolerable.

As the politicians dithered, the problem grew worse. Other nations, especially France, exchanged dollars for gold, building up their reserves. Throughout the 1960s and sitting atop a pile of gold, France called for a return to the gold standard, rather than dependence on the dollar. This tactic was partly inspired by French resentment of American dominance in Europe. By 1968, French officials openly attacked the notion that an ounce of gold was still worth $35.

This caused ripples of unease in markets. In the late 1960s, the U.S. had flooded the world markets with dollars printed to pay for the Vietnam War. Other nations accused the U.S. of exporting inflation, and they chafed at a system that kept everyone in a financial straitjacket except the U.S.

The cracks in the Bretton Woods system could no longer be ignored. Dollars were flowing in Germany, bolstering the mark. The German Central Bank, determined to protect the German export-drive economy, sold marks to keep the currency's value down. But market forces were stronger than the bank. Eventually it stopped trying, and the mark was allowed to gain value. The Dutch followed and allowed their currency to also appreciate.

In August 1971, President Nixon acknowledged that the Bretton Woods system was finished. He announced that the dollar could no longer be exchanged for gold. The "gold window" was closed.

A last-ditch effort was made to save the system when the major powers met in December 1971 in Washington, D.C. to devalue the U.S. dollar against gold and other major currencies. The resulting agreement, called the Smithsonian agreement, was not much of an improvement, despite President Nixon's description of it as the "greatest monetary agreement in the history of the world." Gold was reset at $38 an ounce, and currencies were allowed to fluctuate 2.25 percent, rather than just the 1 percent allowed by Bretton Woods. It was still not enough. The rates proved to be unsustainable. Within a few months, several countries decided to abandon fixed exchange rates and let their currencies float.

However, the decision to devalue the dollar broke the U.S.'s long-standing insistence that $35 would always be worth an ounce of gold. This effectively ended any pretense of a gold standard. In February 1973, the dollar fell 10 percent. The nations of western Europe linked their currencies, allowing a 2.5 percent fluctuation rate, in a system called the snake. They also linked their currencies to the dollar, permitting a 4.5 percent fluctuation rate, in a system called the tunnel.

In hindsight, the end of the Bretton Woods system was predictable. It was necessary to restore confidence in an international economy shattered by war, but the Bretton Woods system could not keep up with how that economy evolved. As European economies found their footing and grew again, the value of their currencies would naturally have to gain against the dollar. The system, however, did not have the flexibility. It was also unable to adapt effectively to changes in how people and institutions handled money. This is an old story—a replay of governments trying to use money for their own ends in the face of what the market wants. The collapse of the gold standard and Bretton Woods meant that markets had regained a measure of control over the value of currencies. Governments, however, would continue to try to direct the market.

It didn't take long for traders to see the potential for profits in this new world of currency trading. Even if the governments could maintain the snake and the tunnel, it still permitted fluctuations—and where there are fluctuations, there's a chance for a profit. In 1971, the International Monetary Market of the Chicago Mercantile Exchange was founded to trade foreign currency futures. Before then, there was little chance to trade currencies except through the banks. A new era had dawned.

This was clear little more than a decade after the collapse of Bretton Woods. The U.S. economy was booming, but the dollar had risen too far too fast. In 1985, the G-5, the most powerful economies in the world—the U.S., Great Britain, France, West Germany, and Japan—sent representatives to a secret meeting at the Plaza Hotel in New York City. The dollar was simply too high, crushing third-world nations under debt and closing American factories because they could not compete with foreign competitors.

Although the meeting was supposedly secret, news of it leaked out, and rumors soon made their way through the markets. In response to reporters' questions, the G-5 released a statement that they would encourage an "appreciation of nondollar currencies." This became known as the "Plaza Accord." Couched in this diplomatic language was the hope that the dollar would decline slowly and in an orderly manner, allowing everyone to adjust to the dollar's new value. But the markets are rarely orderly. Instead of the hoped-for gentle fall, traders punished the dollar, sending it down far faster than anyone had expected. However, the Plaza Accord could rightly be called a success. In the two years after the agreement, the dollar fell more than 30 percent. The U.S. trade deficit narrowed, and the countries met again, this time in Paris, to sign another agreement—the Louvre Accord. This time, the nations agreed to halt the decline of the dollar.

The Rise of the Euro

Although the U.S. dollar has been battered or has fallen in value, its role as the world's reserve currency—the anchor of global commerce—has never been challenged. Until now. The story begins after World War II, when the European nations decided to ensure peace by knitting themselves together.

In 1957, the European Economic Community was established in a landmark treaty signed in Rome. Six countries—France, West Germany, Italy, Belgium, the Netherlands, and Luxembourg—signed the Treaty of Rome. It formed the bedrock of the European Community and was the true beginning of the European Union and the euro.

Several other treaties followed, each one pulling Europe closer together. The Maastricty Treaty, signed in the Dutch city on February 7, 1992, amended the Treaty of Rome and established the European Union, led to the creation of the euro, and established a more cohesive whole that included initiatives on foreign policy and security. The treaty, which called for bold steps to a closer union, was by no means a certain thing. Only 51% of France voted in favor, and Denmark rejected the first version.

Today, however, the euro is circulating in dozens of countries and is used by hundreds of millions of people. If the U.S. dollar is ever unseated as the world's reserve currency, it will be the euro that does it.

The Internet Trade Revolution: Banks Hated It, Speculators Loved It, and the Market Demanded It

In the 1990s, the currency markets grew more sophisticated and faster because money, and how people viewed and used it, was changing. Bankers and merchants have always sought ways to speed up the movement of money. It meant more security, more flexibility, and more profits. A big leap was made with the invention of the telegraph in the 1800s, which allowed people to wire money within a vast network. This first instance of electronic transfer, however, was not commonly used.

After World War II, large numbers of Americans began paying bills with checks rather than with cash. Banks looked for ways to speed up the movement of these payments from the payer to the bank and back to the creditor.

Because sorting and handling bills was relatively inefficient and costly, banks began to turn to a new form of money—electronic. In 1971, the NASDAQ stock exchange opened as a computerized system for selling and buying stocks. By the late 1970s, the banks of the Federal Reserve moved large amounts of money between themselves electronically.

The notion that money was not just a piece of paper, but also something that could assume electronic form, was accepted fitfully by the public. A major advance occurred in 1975, when the government began depositing Social Security checks directly into seniors' accounts. The growth of credit card use also helped.

But it has only been in the past 15 years that the true potential of electronic money has been tapped. The reason is a vastly improved communication infrastructure that has linked the world in a web of fiber-optic cables. This web carries billions of bits of data at the speed of light. More drastic, however, is that the Internet allows anyone to hook into the vast, humming network of communication. Real-time data and general information take the price-discovery process away from interbank control. An individual sitting alone in his home can find at the click of a button an accurate price that only a few years ago would have required an army of traders, brokers, telephones, and squawk boxes. This is the force behind the growing Forex revolution.

These advances in communication came at a time when the former divisions that separated the world into different parts crumbled. The Berlin Wall fell, the Soviet Union collapsed, and hundreds of millions of people joined the liberal, capitalist world, led by the U.S. This process—which has been imperfectly called "globalization"—has been monetary, cultural, and social.

For the foreign exchange markets, everything changed. Currencies that previously had been shut off in totalitarian political systems could be traded. Emerging markets such as those in Southeast Asia flourished, attracting capital and currency speculation.

The 1990s were years of enormous economic growth, but they were also rocked by several crises—in Mexico, in Russia, and in Asia. We will look into the circumstances behind these crises, and what a currency investor can learn from them, later in this book.

What is important to note now is that the speed and ferocity of these crises were unprecedented, and they mark the changes wrought by both technology and the inclusion of societies in the world economic system.

Today, money has moved beyond paper. It exists in bits and bytes, shot around the world at the speed of light. In fact, currency has actually been reduced to a credit instrument, because in retail Forex no actual currency is exchanged. This advance further streamlines the process. But despite the complexity of the international monetary system, it can still be boiled down to one simple transaction—a trade. In currency markets, there must always be a buyer and a seller, a winner and a loser. That partly explains the international appeal of currency trading. People around the world trade, no matter where they live or the style of their society. Virtually everyone inherently understands the currency market. It is one of the oldest forms of the market.

As this chapter has shown, the trade is an ancient and fundamental economic interaction, but the way trades are made today on the modern foreign exchange market is quite new. For most of history, trades were made between two or more people—but usually face to face. Merchants in the eighteenth century gathered in the coffeehouses of London. In New York, traders met under a tree on Wall Street. The telephone changed but did not radically alter this relationship. Orders were carried over the phone, but people still knew the face (or voice) of the person on the other end of the line.

The Internet, which has been used popularly for scarcely a decade, has changed this system completely.

For the first time, relevant information was not posted by weary travelers or executives flying back on Pan Am from the Orient. Individuals and traders could get live data on CNN, Reuters, and Bloomberg. A vast amount of information on markets is now available, often free of charge and easily accessible from home via Internet news sites or 24-hour cable financial news networks. For most of the previous decades, this information was buried in the handwritten ledgers, orders, and charts kept by clerks in giant banks. The banks, naturally, used this information for their own purposes, and in foreign exchange that meant price discovery. They were often the only ones to have an overview of the market, and they made a nice, safe profit. Investors, on the other hand, operated partly in the dark. It took longer for the market to determine an investment's true price. Hence, margins and bid-offer spreads were wide.

The Internet has made it possible for a rumor to spread around the world, and be discredited, within seconds. We are at a turning point in the history of finance. To the average small investor, the workings of high finance have often appeared intimidating, incomprehensible, or inaccessible. Wall Street was an exclusive club in which, by privilege of standing or wealth, favored insiders controlled money and information and made themselves rich.

Small investors were also kept out by relatively high-commission fees to trade through a broker. Now, the Internet provides the same service, virtually for free. The Internet provides rates and price spreads virtually instantaneously, 24 hours a day, seven days a week. Small Order Execution System (SOES) and the dot-com era of the '90s brought Wall Street to Main Street. Everyone from day traders to church groups became experts in U.S. equity markets. Now Forex will introduce the U.S. to the global marketplace.

Seeing the World Through Forex

This chapter opened with a description of the Silk Road 1,000 years ago. A *New York Times* reporter recently visited a city on the old route and wrote of the same mixture of people and goods that had characterized it centuries ago. The patrons who had crowded into local restaurants for dishes of lamb kebab and stew "seem as though they could have been chosen by casually throwing darts at a map of Asia."

"There are alluringly dressed women with black hair, fair skin and striking blue eyes who look passably Russian," wrote the reporter. "There are men with heavily lined, tea-colored faces and brush-thick mustaches who resemble Afghans. There are Turkish-looking Uighurs in Muslim skullcaps and robes and mid-length beards."[4]

Scenes like this are occurring all over the world. Trade is flowing again, released by a communications revolution and new geopolitical realities. Participating in Forex is to join this process, to see the world for the vibrant market that it is. Having an appreciation of this will allow you to see opportunities, anticipate movements, and be a better trader.

Endnotes

1. Weatherford, Jack. *The History of Money.* Three Rivers Press, 1998.

2. Millman, Gregory J. *The Vandal's Crown: How Rebel Currency Traders Overthrew the World's Central Banks.* New York: The Free Press, 1995.

3. Ibid.

4. French, Howard. "Umrumqi Journal; On Old Silk Road, Condos, Mosques and Ethnic Tension." *New York Times*, March 16, 2004.

4

THE BASICS OF FOREIGN EXCHANGE

All Forex investors must master the basic structure and vocabulary of the market before they trade. This chapter introduces and explains some of the basic investing tools and the way they work.

Spot

A spot or Forex transaction is the most basic exchange in the foreign exchange market. It is simply the exchange of one currency for another. Every Forex trade consists of two simultaneous transactions: a buying of one currency and a selling of another. That's why it is called a spot or cash transaction. Technically all transactions have a two-day settlement, except for Canadian transactions, which have a one-day settlement.

For example, one trader exchanges $1 with another trader for 105 yen, just as an American tourist entering Japan exchanges his native currency (U.S. dollars) for the foreign currency (yen).

Overall, the spot market is a very straightforward trading vehicle, and this simplicity has boosted participation in Forex. The only real difference with a tourist transaction is the size difference—which generally starts at $100,000.

Quotes

A Forex transaction can be quoted in either currency, but it must always have two sides. The first currency listed is the *base* currency and is always 1. The second currency listed, also called the *counter* currency, is the amount necessary to buy one unit of the first currency. An example of this is a quote of the U.S. dollar and the Japanese yen at 106, shown as USD/JPY 106. This means that for every U.S. dollar you receive 106 Japanese yen. The U.S. dollar is the base currency, and the yen is the counter currency. Therefore, if the USD/JPY quote moves from 106 to 107, the yen is getting weaker and the dollar stronger. If the quote moves from 106 to 105, the dollar is getting weaker. It's critical to understand the relationship between the base and counter currency.

A quick rule of thumb is that if you trade the base currency, the counter currency executes the reverse. So if you believe the U.S. dollar will gain strength against the Japanese yen, you should buy USD/JPY. This trade buys you U.S. dollars and sells Japanese yen. If you believe the dollar will lose value, you should sell USD/JPY. That sells USD and buys JPY.

Currencies are usually expressed in abbreviated form. Most trading symbols are common sense, but others need to be memorized. Table 4.1 gives an abridged list. The U.S. dollar is USD, the Japanese yen is JPY, the euro is EUR, the British pound sterling is GBP, and the Swiss franc is CHF. A pair could be USD/JPY or EUR/USD, for example.

Table 4.1 Trading Terms

Forex Symbol	Currency Pair	Trading Term
EUR/USD	Euro/U.S. dollar	Euro
GBP/USD	British pound/U.S. dollar	Cable or sterling
USD/JPY	U.S. dollar/Japanese yen	Dollar yen
USD/CHF	U.S. dollar/Swiss franc	Dollar Swiss
USD/CAD	U.S. dollar/Canadian dollar	Dollar Canada
AUD/USD	Australian dollar/U.S. dollar	Aussie dollar or Aussie
EUR/GBP	Euro/British pound	Euro sterling
EUR/JPY	Euro/Japanese yen	Euro yen
EUR/CHF	Euro/Swiss franc	Euro Swiss
GBP/JPY	British pound/Japanese yen	Sterling yen

To truly understand what is occurring in the market, you must have two sides. It not enough to say "the euro is strong" or the "the yen is weak." Rather, you should say "the euro is increasing in value against the yen" or "the yen is decreasing in relative value against the euro." Once you know the currency pair you can establish its relative position.

Also note that you often hear that the dollar is weak or the pound is strong. This is a market generalization based on historic patterns and trading norms. So when you say "the dollar is weak," you are saying that, in general, more U.S. dollars are required to buy another nation's currency than before. You will discover that a lot of Forex is based on the perspective of the person making the comments.

Since the U.S. dollar remains the basis of the global Forex market, it is the universal base for many other currencies. These currencies are commonly expressed in the amount it would take to buy $1. For example, the Swiss franc is often listed as a number such as USD/CHF 1.1700, which means that it takes 1.1700 francs to buy $1. The USD is the base currency, and CHF is the counter. This is referred to as indirect or European terms. However, you sometimes see three liquid currencies that don't obey this rule (and even a few lesser-known ones)—the euro, the British pound, and the Australian dollar. This is referred to as direct or American terms. The euro, for example, may be quoted as EUR/USD 1.21, meaning that it costs $1.21 to buy one euro. There was a time when the British pound occupied a position in the global economy similar to the U.S. dollar's role today.

Currency trades that don't necessarily involve the U.S. dollar are called *cross currencies* or *cross trades*. The same rules apply. AUD/JPY 98.3 indicates that one Australian dollar equals 98.3 Japanese yen.

Majors

These are the most liquid and widely traded currencies in the world. Trades involving majors make up about 90% of total Forex trading. They are USD/JPY, EUR/USD, USD/CHF, AUD/USD, USD/CAN, and GBP/USD.

Cross Rates

A *cross rate* is a currency pair that doesn't involve the USD or the EUR, such as GBP/JPY. Pairs that involve the EUR, such as EUR/JPY or GBP/EUR, are called euro crosses. There are literally hundreds of cross rates. Basically any nation, no matter how obscure, can trade against every other nation's currency. Obscure cross trades are often called "exotic," and traders run the major risk of liquidity. With the increase in Forex trading in recent years, more crosses have been opened for retail trading. This trend will continue.

Pips

The spread is expressed in units called *ticks, points,* or *pips* (an acronym for "price interest point"). A pip is the smallest unit a currency is traded in. It is represented by the last number on the right side of the price. For example, the Japanese yen is calculated to 2 percentage points. A bid/ask quote for the Japanese yen against the U.S. dollar might look like 109.23/28. In this case, the smallest unit is 0.01, which equals one pip. Therefore, the difference between the two figures—0.05—is expressed as five pips. The euro and the pound are both calculated to four decimal points. One pip therefore equals 0.0001 of the currency.

If the Japanese yen climbs from 105.05 to 105.08 against the U.S. dollar, for example, it has gained three pips. If the euro jumps from 1.0032 to 1.0072, it has gained 40 pips.

To calculate how much each pip is actually worth, divide the currency's smallest tradeable unit by the currency exchange rate. Let's take the EUR/USD as an example. The euro's smallest tradeable unit is 0.0001, and the currency exchange rate with the U.S. dollar is 0.88. To determine each pip's value, calculate 0.0001/0.88, which equals 0.000113.

Bid/Ask

Forex has a buy (*bid*) price and a sell (*offer*) price. If you've been in a foreign country and exchanged money at a kiosk, you've probably noticed a board displaying each currency with two prices. Only a small amount separates them in value. The higher price is the offer price—the amount someone or an institution is asking to sell a currency. The other, lower price is the bid price—the amount someone or an institution is offering to buy a currency. This is no different on a retail Forex screen. The market maker shows a buy/sell or two-sided price, which is the price it is willing to deal on. The difference between the two prices is called the *spread,* which is expressed in pips. The spread is a function of market conditions and liquidity. Spread rates have tightened significantly over the last few years thanks to increased competition, information flows, and technology. Most Forex firms now offer three-pip spreads on the majors and five on everything else.

Lot

A *lot* is a standardized trading unit of 1,000 USD, leveraged 100 to 1, controlling $100,000 USD units of base currency. It has no expiration or time restraints due to the automatic rollover policy.

Mini Lot

A *mini lot* is a standardized trading unit of 100 USD, leveraged 100 to 1, controlling $10,000 worth of base currency. A mini lot is one-tenth of a standard lot.

Basic Tools of Trading

Each investor has several tools available when trading Forex.

Positions

Trading Forex is probably the easiest way to execute and monitor profit and loss (P/L) in the investment community. Every position consists of a *long* and a *short*—a buying of one currency in a pair and the selling of another.

One advantage of Forex is that there is no restriction on short-selling a currency pair, because every trade is made up of a buy and a sell. In fact, there are no real restrictions or limits that stop a trader from executing any trade. As long as there is liquidity in a currency pair and a willing counterparty, a trade can be made.

Market Order

A *market order* is an order to buy or sell a currency at the current market price. In basic terms, you see favorable numbers and make a trade. Market orders, however, do not guarantee that the trade will be made according to the numbers you saw. In fast-moving markets such as Forex, the position may change before the order is carried out. In other cases, the quotes may not be exactly accurate, because the Forex market has so many players.

Limit Order

A *limit order* allows an investor to avoid buying or selling a currency at a price higher or lower than the investor wants. In this case, a limit order may be more effective than a market order, which will be executed at whatever price is available. A buy limit order can only be executed at the limit price or lower, and a sell limit order can only be executed at the limit price or higher.

For example, in a wild market, you might send in an order to buy Japanese yen for 120.5 and end up with 121 because the market shifted before your trade was executed. To avoid this, you can submit a limit order that says you will buy Japanese yen at any price up to 120.5. If the price of the Japanese yen breaks that barrier, your trade is not executed, offering you a measure of protection. Be aware that some brokers may charge more for a limit order than for a market order.

GTC (good till canceled) is a type of limit order that remains active until the trader decides to cancel the order. It is the trader's responsibility to monitor the order because the dealer will not cancel the order at any time.

GFD (good for the day) is a type of limit order that remains active until the end of the day, at which point the dealer automatically removes it.

Stop Order

With a *stop order,* an investor sets a price that will automatically trigger a trade. When the price is hit, the stop order becomes a market order to either buy or sell. Stops are typically used by investors as a safeguard to lock in a profit or to limit losses.

For example, suppose you make a USD/JPY trade at 120 and it suddenly moves to 118. According to your strategy, the yen will gain value to 115, so you don't want to liquidate your position.

Instead, you buy a stop order for 118.5. If the yen loses value and drifts back up to 120, your stop order executes a trade automatically, protecting your profit.

The danger with stop orders is that the markets might jump around and trigger your stops prematurely. Let's say the yen rises to 118, falls back to 119, and then resumes its gain to 115. Your position has already been liquidated at 118.5 when the yen hit your stop.

Also be aware that a stop order doesn't guarantee that you will receive the price at which you set the stop. When the stop is hit, it becomes a market order, which means you are at the market makers' mercy regarding best price execution. And, in a rapidly moving market, this best price can be well off from your desired price. Because stops are a critical tool to a Forex trader, particular attention should be paid to the firm's exact policy to stops.

Order Cancels Other

Order Cancels Other (OCO) is a highly effective order in the Forex trader's toolbox. It is a mixture of two limit and/or stop orders. Two orders are placed with price variables above and below the current market value. When one order is executed, the other is automatically removed.

This trading technique can be used when trading around support and resistance. Suppose a trader believes that the EUR/USD resistance at 130.00 will break the trend and continue upward, but if it holds the price will move to 129.00. Say the current market is at 129.90. The trader places one buy limit order at 130.05 (above resistance) and the sell limit order at 129.45, below the minor support. If the market breaks 130.05, the buy is executed and the sell limit is removed.

Stop-Limit Order

This order combines the features of the stop order and limit order. If you have a stop, but are worried that the market might move too fast before the order is executed, you can include a limit order as well. Once the price triggers the stop, it doesn't become a market order—it becomes a limit order. If the market moves beyond your desired price, the limit order prevents the trade from being made in the first place. But be careful when entering these orders. There is a chance they may get triggered prematurely, causing you to miss the market.

Rollovers

When an investor buys a currency on the spot market, he doesn't actually take possession of the currency—no more than a trader in corn futures has bushels of corn delivered to his doorstep. A spot purchase does, however, call for the currency to be delivered within two days. But instead of having the currency actually delivered to an investor's account, it's reset, or *rolled over*. In this way, a retail Forex position can be held indefinitely.

The account may also fluctuate because of interest differential payments. For positions open at 5 p.m. EST there is a daily rollover (interest payment) that you either pay or earn on an open position, generally depending on your established currency pair, margin level, and interest rate differential. If you do not want to earn or pay interest on your positions, simply make sure that they are closed at 5 p.m. EST, the established end of the market day.

The exact time of each rollover depends on the trading platform. Each platform is different, and you should investigate the rollover time before trading, but most rollovers occur each day at 5 p.m. New York time.

If you made a trade on Monday morning London time, at 5 p.m. New York time, your trade would be rolled over. And this would occur every day after that. Tuesday at 5 p.m., Wednesday at 5 p.m.—as long as you are in position before 5 p.m., every time the clock hits 4:59 p.m., your trade rolls over.

Understanding rollovers is critical to understanding Forex. You don't want one million Japanese yen delivered to your account or to be pulled from a trade prematurely. Therefore, you need a rollover to maintain your position. Retail platforms today perform rollovers almost seamlessly, so your trades can stay in the market for virtually any amount of time.

All retail Forex platforms automatically roll over open positions to the next settlement date. Without the rollover, speculation in Forex would be obsolete except for short-term (day) trading.

The reason rollovers take place at 5 p.m. New York time is that 5 p.m. is considered the beginning of the international trading day. This is when the market opens in Singapore.

But if your trade includes a time period that falls over the weekend, you have a three-day rollover. This is how interest is calculated over weekends: On Wednesday at 5 p.m. in New York, the sum of three days of interest is added to or subtracted from the account. These three-day rollovers offset trades that would occur throughout the weekend.

Interest Rate Differentials, or Rollover Charge

Rollover interest varies depending on the currency. Fundamentally, interest becomes a factor because in Forex you lend one currency and borrow another. Say a trader takes a position of buying GBP/USD. He is actually credited in carrying pounds by borrowing dollars. Therefore, you have a bank account of pounds receiving the pound interest rate and paying the lending cost of the dollars.

The interest rate is determined by the overnight lending rates (London Interbank Offered Rates [LIBOR]), or a derivative, for each currency in the pair. This is one major reason why the role of central banks is so important to the currency markets.

For example, the U.S. Federal Reserve has maintained a prime rate of 2 percent, while the Bank of England has a 4 percent rate, making the respective LIBOR rates the same for illustration purposes. That is a large spread between the two currencies' overnight yields. Every day you hold this long GBP/USD position, you receive 2 percent on the total amount traded. To earn this interest, you need to keep a margin of at least 2 percent. Forex Capital Markets (FXCM) charges or pays out interest on a per-lot basis. Any position that is smaller borrows funds from FXCM, and FXCM keeps the interest to compensate for the added risk and service associated with lending funds. The exact rollover procedures are at the discretion of the individual clearing firms, and they should be researched very carefully.

Here is an example of the calculations for interest differential on any particular day:

EUR/USD 0.25 (2.0% – 1.75% = .25%)

EUR/GBP 1.5 points

The formulas are calculated as follows:

EUR/GBP = .00015 × 100,000 = 15.00

15.00 / 1.8925 = $7.93

For most short-term Forex trading, the interest rate differential is inconsequential because the trades exit the market before rollover can affect the trade. The inherent volatility of the trade outweighs any benefit or loss that can be incurred. But for longer-term positions, the starting interest rate should be considered.

Leverage

Leverage allows an investor to use an amount of money to raise a far larger quantity. Therefore, it should not be taken lightly. In Forex, leverage can transform $1,000 into $100,000 on the markets. The initial amount of money, called a *margin,* allows the investor to leverage a much larger investment.

This means that even the smallest investor can suddenly command large positions in the Forex market. Leverage, however, can be extremely dangerous. Just as it allows investors to realize much larger gains over a very short time, it can also lead to staggering losses.

For example, you can buy currency on margin by putting up $1,000 and borrowing $100,000 to purchase a total of $101,000 worth of contracts. In this case, you are leveraged 100 to 1. Let's say, for example, that your position increases 15 percent to about $115,000. You can sell, pay back the $100,000, and keep your $14,000, minus some expenses. Your initial $1,000 yielded $14,000—a return of 1,300 percent when the position rose only 15 percent.

But let's take a look at what happens if your position falls 15 percent. Now your position is worth only about $85,000, and you still owe $100,000. The $15,000 difference is now a loss of more than 1,300 percent. You will also pay interest on the loan, which decreases your potential return and increases your potential loss.

However, things rarely work out this way because of margin calls. Each investor buying on leverage must maintain a minimum amount in his or her account called the margin.

Because of the potential for destabilizing losses, the retail Forex market has automatic stops that close an account if the position falls below the amount in the margin.

Still, I advise you not to over-leverage. One mistake investors make is leveraging their account too high by trading much larger sizes than their account should prudently trade. A further effect of over-leverage is that an investor may have to withdraw from his position before his strategy calls for it.

However, read the fine print in all trading agreements. In most instances if market conditions change dramatically, the trader on the firm is responsible for all losses. Any guaranteed stops should be investigated and directly questioned.

In most markets leverage is an afterthought, but in Forex it is the foundation of the industry. Without it, retail Forex operational costs would shut out small investors. Remember that every transaction has an operational cost. If a firm makes only 10 cents per trade, that won't cover the costs. But by trading on margin, the firm can recoup. A trade leveraged 10 to 1 is worth $1; 100 to 1, $10. What about 300? That's a 30-pip profit. If a firm can get between the three-to-four-pip spread, it can realize hefty gains on every trade. Unfortunately, Forex firms encourage investors to use a great amount of leverage—not to give the investor an advantage, but because it is more profitable in the short run for the Forex firm.

Controlling Leverage

Although the lure of leverage might be appealing to new investors looking for the big score, you should use this instrument carefully. Remember that it takes only a small position on the right side, given the volatility, to make some significant returns. An investor should look at his or her entire risk capital and trading strategy and then make leverage decisions.

Initial Margin

The *initial margin* is the amount of cash a trader must deposit, usually with a broker, to begin trading futures. The initial margin is held to guarantee that the terms of the contract are fulfilled.

Margin Call

If you are trading futures and your position declines, you may be asked to cover your losses by depositing money to maintain a minimum balance. This requirement is called the *margin call*. For example, if the broker has a $1,000 initial margin and your position falls 10 percent, he might ask you for another $100 to cover the decline. Brokers typically give clients between two and five days to cover the call. In some cases, however, the broker might exercise his or her right to simply sell the position, giving the client no time to cover the call. After all, if you are trading on leverage, the broker has loaned you a lot of money, and he or she will do what is necessary to protect it.

Commissions

If there is one thing investors and traders seem to know, it's this: don't get gouged by commissions. Earning a return is difficult enough, but giving extra points to a broker can often mean the difference between good and mediocre performance.

In the Forex market, however, you should get used to the fact that you will be paying some kind of commission, even to "no commission" brokers. Every currency trade has a spread, which can be several pips and is included in the trade. Depending on the size of the trade, this spread can cost $10 to $40 per trade. A trader should be very aware of the cost of the spread to their overall strategy.

You might often hear that the Forex market is "no-commission," but this is simply not true. In investments, there are no free lunches. The introductory broker (IB) or futures commission merchant (FCM) might not charge any upfront fees, but the fees are hidden in the spread. The FCM makes money between the bid/ask spread. Even the spread can be deliberately widened to give pips to the IB. And the IB receives a "rebate" from the FCM, which is part of the spread. The appeal of "no commission" can be deceiving and can cause investors to pick the wrong trading firm to work with. A firm that charges a fixed fee might provide tighter spreads and therefore cost the investor less than a firm with wide spreads.

So when you are shopping around for a broker or an FCM (a fuller discussion of this position and its role is given later), don't be distracted by offers of "commission-free" trading. Instead, consider what you are paying for and what you are getting. This might depend on your personal investment style. Do you like a lot of services? Be prepared to pay for them. But if that's what makes you comfortable and allows you to execute profitable trades, it's worth it.

Graphic: Calculations for the Spot Market

The spot market deals in very small units. Profits and losses are usually measured in decimal points.

For example, the value of a USD/JPY position at the open is calculated this way:

Buy one unit of USD/JPY at 120.00

100,000 USD (one unit) × 120.00 = 12,000,000 yen

At the close:

Sell one unit of USD/JPY at 120.2

100,000 USD (one unit) × 120.2 = 12,020,000 yen

The position made is 20,000 yen, which in U.S. dollars is 20,000 / 120.2 = $166.39.

The value of a USD/EUR position at the open is calculated this way:

Buy one unit of USD/EUR at 0.8022

100,000 USD (one unit) × 0.8022 = 80,220 euros

At the close:

Sell one unit of USD/EUR at 0.8058

100,000 USD (one unit) × 0.8058 = 80,580 euros

The position made is 360 euros, which in U.S. dollars is 360 / .8058 = $446.76.

The value of a GPB/JPY position at the open is calculated this way:

Buy one unit of GPB/JPY at 160.83

100,000 GPB (one unit) × 160.83 = 16,083,000 yen

At the close:

Sell one unit of GPB/JPY at 159.03

100,000 GBP (one unit) × 159.03 = 15,903,000 yen

The position lost is 180,000 yen, which in British pounds is 180,000 / 159.03 = 1,131.86 pounds.

Forex Regulators

No overarching global agency is responsible for regulating the activity of Forex markets. Regulation is left up to each country. Some countries take a hands-off approach to regulations. Others, like the U.S. and England, have jumped in with both feet.

SFBC

The Swiss Federal Banking Commission supervises areas of the financial sector in Switzerland.

IDAC

The Investment Dealers Association of Canada is a national self-regulatory organization.

SFC

The Securities and Futures Commission of Hong Kong has jurisdiction over leveraged foreign exchange trading in that city.

FSA

The Financial Service Authority of the UK is an independent, non-governmental body that has regulated the financial services industry in the UK since 2000. It was given its present-day authority by the Financial Services and Markets Act of 2000.

ASIC

This is the Australian Securities and Investment Commission.

CFTC and NFA

In the U.S., the Federal Reserve Bank monitors the banking system. The Commodity Futures Trading Commission (CFTC) has jurisdiction over futures and, recently, the Forex markets.

The government agency CFTC monitors the National Futures Association's (NFA) activities. The CFTC has limited regulatory authority over retail over-the-counter (OTC) Forex markets in the U.S. But although no single entity in the U.S. has direct regulatory oversight in the Forex market, the CFTC has effectively begun to take on that role.

The Commodity Exchange Act (CEA) gave the CFTC the authority to regulate the sale of OTC Forex futures and options to retail clients only if the counterparty is a regulated entity. Regulated entities include banks, financial institutions, broker-dealers, and FCMs. By limiting the parties regulated entities can interact with, the CFTC has exerted some level of control. The CFTC has the authority to shut down unregulated Forex entities—specifically, FCMs. (Also, the CEA has a provision for any violation regarding antifraud and antimanipulation connected with OTC Forex transactions in the retail market.)

Despite the reputation that markets dislike regulation, this has not been the case with Forex. Most Forex firms have embraced the new regulatory authority because it gives them legitimacy and helps weed out fraudulent players in the Forex markets.

NFA

Since the CFTC is a government agency, it does not issue actual rules for Forex transactions. It gave that right to the NFA. The NFA is a U.S.-based, industry-wide, self-regulating organization. The NFA was formed to provide regulatory programs, oversight, and market integrity primarily to the futures market but has now entered Forex as well. Basically the NFA makes the rules that govern the Forex market—but remember, rules are not laws.

Today, anyone who participates in the Forex markets should deal only with firms that have some level of NFA designation. Although the NFA has done an impressive job of convincing a majority of the industry to register with the organization, not all firms are members. Technically, these firms are unregulated, so I advise you to avoid them. Determining whether a firm complies with the NFA should be an elemental part of your background research.

On December 1, 2003, the NFA was given enormous authority to regulate the Forex market with the "Forex Transaction with Forex Dealer Member Interpretive Notice."

Effective December 1, 2003

"The Commodity Futures Modernization Act of 2000 (CFMA), which was signed into law on December 21, 2000, amended the Commodity Exchange Act (CEA) to provide that only certain regulated entities may offer off-exchange foreign currency futures and options contracts (forex) to retail customers. Under the CFMA, registered futures commission merchants (FCMs) and their affiliates are among the entities that may offer forex contracts to retail customers. As described below, NFA Bylaw 306 creates a Forex Dealer Member category for certain NFA Members who act as counterparties to forex transactions with retail customers. This category allows NFA to exercise appropriate regulatory jurisdiction over the retail forex activities of these Members without imposing unnecessary, and potentially duplicative, regulatory burdens on Members that are otherwise subject to regulatory oversight for their activities."

Forex Designations

Forex Dealer Members

These individuals literally make the Forex market. Without them there would be no trading opportunity for the retail investor. They extend the credit, handle clearing, back officer operations, and provide an orderly market for investors.

A Forex dealer combines the roles of a market maker and specialist in the equity market. The primary role of the market maker is to provide liquidity through tradeable prices to the market. The specialist's role is to intervene in the market when temporary price disparity occurs. Forex market makers provide liquidity and maintain an orderly market. When a retail trader sees a quote on his or her screen, it is coming directly from the Forex dealer member, and that person functions as the counterparty.

Retail Forex traders do not trade directly in the traditional interbank market, even though many Forex firms claim their clients do. A trader is dealing in the interbank market if the counterparty is one of the major global financial institutions with trades starting at one million. Retail traders, however, have neither the trading volume nor the credit rating to trade on the interbank. That's what makes them retail traders. What the retail trader is trading in is a limited offshoot of the larger interbank market.

In today's competitive retail environment, traders trade on quotes closely mirroring interbank prices provided by their Forex firms. Each Forex firm receives prices from outside providers such as EBS or Reuters or the banks the firm trades with. Most larger Forex firms trade on the interbank market with banks such as Deutsche Bank, HSBC, and JP Morgan.

Each Forex firm has a market maker who reviews the feeds from outside agencies and creates a price to offer to its clients. This is Forex market making.

One of the supposed advantages of the Forex market is its liquidity. But perhaps this liquidity is just a mirage—as was recently addressed by some major financial institutions at the FX Week 2004 Congress. First, the Forex retail dealer has no fiduciary or legally binding obligation to provide liquidity and an orderly market in extreme conditions. In fact, most FCMs specifically address this in their account-opening documents. In extreme market conditions, the retail trader is vulnerable because he is dealing with a single counterparty. If the counterparty doesn't offer the retail trader executable prices, he is stuck. The second reason, which is a major concern for the interbank participants, is that the amount of leverage extended to retail traders soon outpaces actual trading activity. This is not a major concern as long as buyers and sellers are relatively balanced. If they get out of balance, however, there could be a significant liquidity crisis.

Some conflicts arise in this process. Because the trader can deal with only one counterparty, he is limited to accepting the price (or not trading) and is subject to the firm's ability to trade. But the dealer knows the trader's position and account information, often making it easy to figure out his next trade. This gives the market maker a significant advantage. Strange spike-hitting stop orders can make the trader think. In addition, this mechanism gives the Forex firm's market makers flexibility in providing quotes.

Futures Commission Merchants

Firms that act as Forex member dealers must be registered as futures commission merchants (FCMs). In the U.S., the FCM is the market maker in the retail Forex world. The CFTC and NFA have strict requirements for all FCMs, such as adequate capitalization and antifraud and ethical provisions, that are not dissimilar to the rules that brokers and dealers operate under in securities.

On this single issue I will make an unreserved judgment: *Do not trade* with any retail Forex firm in the U.S. that doesn't have this designation.

Introductory Brokers

An introductory broker (IB) is a Forex broker who provides advice and technical support. He refers the actual trade execution and floor operations to an FCM. An IB cannot make a market by himself; he relies on an FCM for price and execution. The IB is focused on his clients, whereas the FCM focuses on the trading operations and market making. Generally, an IB works with a single futures commission merchant, so the client is limited in market depth and execution options. IBs are not allowed to hold funds in any manner, so all funding must be done through the IB's FCM. Choosing an IB depends on the type of trading, the amount of assistance and support required, and the ability to watch and execute your trades.

An IB must register with the NFA and pass the series 3 or series 7 exam.

Commodity Trading Advisers

A commodity trading adviser (CTA) is an expert in trading commodities and futures contracts. You can go to a CTA for advice and strategy tips for your portfolio, which may be the best way to learn about trading futures. You can develop a one-on-one relationship, which may prove to be the most effective way to learn about Forex trading. Each CTA must register with the NFA and pass a series 3 or series 7 exam.

Brokers

In most markets the broker acts as an intermediary who matches buyers and sellers. For this, he earns a commission. However, the broker, in the pure sense of the word, is not an important part of the retail Forex market. Investors deal directly with the market maker or dealer. Although this process might lower transaction costs, it ultimately hurts the individual's investing returns because a trader is limited to the quotes on his or her retail platform. In the retail Forex market, an IB or FCM representative fills the role of the broker.

These entities have limited use because the broker can trade with only a single market maker, acting as a price taker, while the FCM is the counterparty to all trades. This is one of the major flaws of the current Forex trading mechanism. In addition, until recently, no educational requirement or official registration was needed to go into business as a broker or FCM in Forex.

Managed Accounts

Managed accounts are the watered-down Forex version of a mutual fund, without the rigid structure. An investor gives trading discretion to an individual or firm to trade an account on their behalf. This is a viable solution for individuals looking to diversify into Forex without hands-on involvement. It's an effective way for retail investors to benefit from the knowledge, resources, and experience of an investment manager without the restrictions of investing in a hedge fund or other alternative investment. From a manager's perspective it allows them to create a semi-structured product without all the headaches of outside regulation.

An investor simply chooses a particular manager or trading strategy and opens an account with the corresponding firm.

Investors choosing this route, however, should be very careful. In the U.S., managed accounts don't have to register as a separate investment product with the SEC, and if they stay within the Forex market, no disclosure documents are needed. Managers don't have to disclose strategy, an audited performance, fees, or anything else required to help an investor make an educated investment decision. If a managed account traded futures, the manager would be required under CFTC/NFA guidelines to develop and present a disclosure document to potential investors. In this document you would find personal and corporate biographies, compiled or audited performance, risk disclosure, and an overview of the trading strategy—in short, enough information to make an educated decision. In addition, there must be a registration as a CTA, CPO or registered investment advisor (RIA), which has filing and education requirements.

To participate in a managed account, an investor must sign separate documents along with the standard account-opening forms. These documents allow the manager to trade on each client's behalf (called *limited discretion*) and let the manager withdraw predetermined fees. However, it does not give the manager full discretion to control all funds. A manager trades through a bank or FCM and directs the client to open an account with that firm. According to the NFA, a manager can charge at most a 2 percent management fee and 20 percent of returns, and he or she must disclose any other compensation derived from that account.

Interview with the National Futures Association

The National Futures Association (NFA) is a not-for-profit membership corporation formed in 1976 to become the futures industry's self-regulatory organization. The first NFA regulatory operations began on October 1, 1982. Today, the organization, among other tasks, audits members to enforce compliance with NFA financial requirements. The NFA regulates several Forex participants. In this interview, Kathryn Page Camp, associate general counsel of the NFA, answers questions about the organization.

How did the NFA get involved with Forex?
We got involved after the Commodity Futures Modernization Act (CFMA) was enacted. The act tried to clarify jurisdiction. It said you can only do retail Forex if you're in one of these categories, and we listed a number of categories. One of them was futures commission merchant (FCM). This is the category these firms were registering in in order to do Forex business with retail

customers. And if you are an FCM, you are required to be an NFA member. So we were concerned there was nobody who could regulate the transactions of these firms getting into the business of FCM. Since they were members, we decided that we should regulate their Forex business as well.

In layman's terms, can you break down exactly who is regulated by the NFA and the Commodity Futures Trading Commission (CFTC) and who is still outside its jurisdiction?

First let me discuss the Commodity Futures Trading Commission. The Commodity Exchange Act says that if you do retail Forex, you have to be a regulated entity or an affiliate. The unregulated entities outside the jurisdiction are banks, insurance companies, broker/dealers (although there is a lot of crossover between them). FCMs are within the Commodity Futures Trading Commission jurisdiction. The provisions within the CFMA only give the CFCT the ability to put firms out of business if they are not in one of those regulated categories or take an antifraud action or antimanipulation action against an FCM or affiliate. That's all the CFTC has jurisdiction over, basically. They cannot, however, write rules.

The NFA actually has broader ability to regulate. Once someone becomes an NFA member, their relationship with us is by contract, where they agree to abide by our rules, so we are not limited by what the CFMA or CFTC says. We can write rules to govern any of their conduct. And we can actually reach areas besides fraud. So right now we are regulating areas such as capital requirements, supervision, salutation, promotional materials, knowing their customer. It's a broader spectrum of rules.

The mandatory registration of FCMs gives the NFA the ability to regulate, and since any entity conducting business with an FCM must be registered, they are therefore governed by the NFA within the U.S.

Exactly how has the Commodity Futures Modernization Act made Forex trading safer for the retail investor?

The CFMA made trading safer for individual investors because it prohibited unregulated firms from selling Forex to retail investors and because it gave the Commodity Futures Trading Commission the authority to take antifraud actions against many of the firms that are authorized to sell these products to retail investors. NFA's rules prohibit fraud, but they also impose affirmative obligations on Forex dealer members that are designed to 1) ensure that retail customers understand the risks and the costs involved in trading these products, 2) protect retail customers against unethical business practices, and 3) require Forex dealer members to have adequate capital for their business, which reduces (but does not eliminate) the risk that customers will lose their funds due to bankruptcy or other reasons unrelated to the customer's market losses.

There has been some criticism of the NFA that they are only regulating for capitalization and massive fraud. What is the NFA game plan in regulating areas such as market making and trading?

Well, first I need to stress that Forex is a fairly new area of regulation. These firms are not used to being regulated. They and we are still in the learning process. Our general approach is to start with education. If we see something wrong we would rather point it out to our members to get them to correct it, to help them understand what the rules and guidelines really are. We don't start, except in extreme situations of fraud, with action. But we do look at all those things. We have done a lot with education, and we are now at the point where you will be seeing a lot of action, starting with marketing and promotional materials.

Would you say that now the NFA is moving into an action phase?

Yes. Our rules have been in effect since December 2003, which has given our members plenty of time to become educated. Now we are looking to enforce.

What about the problem of global jurisdiction? Is the NFA working with any other international regulatory bodies to regulate Forex?

We do have some working relationships with foreign FROs [future readiness officers], but we really haven't done much to coordinate regulations. We have worked with Taiwan as they develop their Forex regulations. Where we coordinate more is if we find something going on with international implications from an enforcement perspective.

What legal obligation do dealer member firms (FCMs) have to provide an orderly market?

There are no rules specifically requiring FCMs to provide an orderly market in off-exchange Forex. Both the CEA and NFA Compliance Rule 2-36 prohibit fraud and manipulation, and some failures to provide an orderly market may involve fraud or manipulation. In addition, NFA Compliance Rule 2-36 prohibits Forex dealer members from engaging in conduct that is inconsistent with just and equitable principles of trade, and our interpretive notice requires them to quote both the bid and ask. These requirements impose an indirect obligation on Forex dealer members. However, there are no documents (that I'm aware of) that describe a firm's obligation to provide an orderly market.

What recourse does a retail trader have against abuse?

If they are NFA members, we do have an arbitration program to recover money lost. We can also take an enforcement action that won't get them their money back but might give them the satisfaction of protecting other customers down the road.

Would it make sense for a $500 transaction, or does it have to be larger?

$500 is not likely to be cost-effective, since there are arbitration fees involved. [It might be] if fraud was involved. On the other hand, it doesn't have to be $50,000. We have many claims for $5,000 and $10,000.

A person wanting to make a claim can call us directly or use our electronic filing system. You can go on our website (www.nfa.futures.org) and can find the forms to file. There are electronic forms as well as arbitration rules and procedures.

Can you give any overall advice to retail traders?

Before they do any investing, they should do their homework. If it is not a bank or an insurance company or broker dealer, or if they are touting themselves as an NFA member, check up on the claim.

5

FOREX TRADING VEHICLES

As the largest market in the world, Forex attracts all kinds of investors. Each has a different reason for being in the market, and each uses a different technique and mechanism to achieve his or her investing goals. Although you might not be interested in using these techniques or strategies yourself, it's a good idea to learn about them anyway. They will move the markets and affect your returns.

Most traders in the Forex market today have one ambition—to make money fast. Of the market's average daily turnover—$1.2 trillion—more than 90 percent of the trades are speculative. That means that the person or institution investing that money has no other objective than to turn a profit. This is supported by other

Forex statistics. More than 40 percent of Forex trades last less than two days, and 80 percent last less than two weeks (source: BIS Triennial Survey, 2001).

Other participants in the market, however, are concerned less with making money than with protecting it. They want to hedge against currency swings or manage cash flow across international borders. They include giant banks, insurance companies, and multinational corporations such as BMW, Sony, and Wal-Mart, which must report profits from countries all over the world.

These players can select from several different kinds of trading vehicles to best realize their trading strategy and achieve their investing objective.

The most widely used vehicle is the *spot market,* also called *cash* or simply *Forex.* Spot trading represents the most basic transaction in Forex. A buyer and seller agree on a price and exchange money within two days. Deal done. Spot, however, is not the only trading tool available to investors. As in other markets, alternative investing vehicles were developed to satisfy each participant's unique needs.

These trading tools—called *derivatives*—are *forwards, futures, and options* and *swaps.* The last two are derivatives that have become critical players in the foreign exchange market. Of the Forex market's daily turnover in 2001, about $650 million was swaps, almost $400 million was spot transactions, and more than $100 million was forwards.

Each Forex participant can select the vehicle that best suits his or her purpose. For example, Ford Motor Company uses a forward to stabilize its cash flow in foreign revenues. Citibank might prefer a swap to lower its exposure to a specific currency. A hedge fund might select options to take advantage of currency moves.

A good way to understand the concept of choosing an investment instrument is to compare trading to a journey. Anyone planning to travel from, say, Boston to Mexico City can choose from a variety of transportation methods. You can fly, drive, take a train, or even walk. No method is necessarily wrong, but perhaps some ways are better than others. It all depends on what you want out of the trip.

When developing a trading strategy, you should see foreign exchange not as a single trading vehicle but as one with many choices. Once you have determined a strategy, it's critical that you choose a trading vehicle that will get you to your destination most effectively. Forex is just one way to trade foreign exchange.

Forwards and Futures

A *forward* is a trade in which the delivery of the currency is set for a specific date in the future. Typical forward contracts are one, two, three, six, or 12 months in length.

Traders sometimes use forwards to take advantage of the difference between interest rates in different countries. If the European Central Bank's (ECB) interest rate is five percent and the U.S.'s is three percent, a trader might convert his or her dollars into euros to gain the higher return offered by the ECB. At the same time, however, the trader could also buy dollars forward for delivery some time in the future, thus locking in the favorable exchange. When the trader delivers the contract, he has more dollars left over.

Of course, it's not that easy to make money. The difference in interest rates is factored into most forward contracts by the market. Thus, a forward price may be cheaper or more expensive than the current spot price, depending on interest rates. Continuing with the preceding example, a forward contract for euros would be more expensive because of the superior rate of return available in Europe. This higher price is called a *premium*. A cheaper price is called a *discount*.

The value of a forward, therefore, is not calculated by the market's anticipation of how much one currency is worth compared to another, but rather the difference in the interest rates of both countries.

A *currency future*, like a forward, is an agreement between a buyer and a seller to trade a currency at a certain price on a specified date in the future. The primary difference between a forward and a future is that a future is traded on a regulated exchange, but a forward is not.

Futures are not new to the markets. They were developed centuries ago to protect businesses from fluctuations in prices by transferring the risk to speculators. Hedgers can be businesses that want to protect themselves from price gyrations in materials they rely on. For example, a baker might need to buy grain every year at a certain price. He might buy a grain future, thus protecting himself if a storm wipes out most of the crop and makes the price of grain skyrocket.

Speculators are on the other side of the hedge. They hope to make money if the price of the underlying commodity fluctuates in their favor. Using the same example of the baker, let's say the weather is exceptionally good, the grain crop is huge, and the price falls because there's so much grain on the market. The baker has already agreed to buy the grain at a higher price, so the speculator makes money on the difference between the two prices.

The baker would rather have the security of knowing that he has access to grain at a certain price instead of waiting to see what the market delivers, good or bad. Speculators, on the other hand, absorb that risk and get a chance to make money. In this sense, speculators play a critically important role in the economy. They provide a kind of insurance to the markets that protects corporations and individuals and encourages stability and innovation.

It makes sense that futures were first offered for currencies in 1972, when currencies were allowed to float against the U.S. dollar. (For a full discussion of those events, see Chapter 3, "The History of Forex (and Why You Should Care).") Transnational corporations were suddenly exposed to swings in currency values that could wreak havoc on their carefully planned business operations and balance sheets.

Futures contracts are typically traded over an exchange (exchange-traded contracts). To buy a future, an individual or corporation posts a small amount of cash as a *margin* or a bond.

The price of futures fluctuates depending on market conditions. If events cause the market to believe that a currency will rise in value over the next year, a contract that locks in a lower price will be worth more. The difference between the future price and the market price is settled at the end of each business day. This difference is added to (or subtracted from) the margin. Losses on the margin must be replenished, or the market participant's position is closed.

Currency futures were first offered on the Chicago Mercantile Exchange (CME) in 1972. (Before then, the CME specialized in offering futures for commodities such as grain, pork, and orange juice.) Today, a full range of futures is available at the CME 24 hours a day via the GlobeEx trading platform.

Options

Options, like futures, came into existence to help institutions and companies cope with increased fluctuations in the foreign exchange markets. Investors who buy options have the right, if they choose, to buy a specific amount of currency at a set price on or before a specific date. At its most fundamental level, an option is a choice.

Options are an effective hedging device against currency fluctuations. They allow a buyer to lock in an exchange rate and then use the option only if the situation warrants it. The buyer, however, must pay a premium at the outset for an option.

A good way to understand options is to read a legend about their first use. An ancient Greek philosopher, Thales of Miletus, grew sick of jibes that he was a poor man. Thales insisted he was poor because he chose to be, and one year he decided to prove it.

That year, Thales determined from the weather patterns that the olive crop would be especially large. In the off-season before the harvest, Thales went to the olive press owners and offered a deal. He would pay them a small amount in advance for the exclusive right to operate their presses during the harvest if he wanted to. If he didn't use the presses, the press owners could keep the advance. If he did, the press owners would receive the guaranteed rate. The press owners liked the idea, and Thales soon had a monopoly on the presses. As it turned out, Thales's prediction was correct. The olive growers reaped a bountiful harvest, and when they went to rent presses, they found that Thales controlled them all. He could charge whatever rate he wanted to. Using an ancient version of options, Thales had demonstrated that he could be rich if he wanted to.[1]

Options, like every other foreign currency transaction, involve a person who is buying a currency and another who is selling it. The right to buy a currency is a *call option,* and the right to sell it is a *put option.* Each option is both a call and a put. Therefore, an option to buy euros and sell U.S. dollars is a euro call and a U.S. dollar put.

Investors who use options tend to be institutions that rely on stable currency exchange rates to operate. This includes banks, multinational corporations, importers and exporters, and investors in foreign stock exchanges. On the other side of the deal are speculators who, as they do in futures, assume risk in the hopes of making a profit.

Options provide investors with a relatively cheap way to hedge themselves against risk when trading foreign currencies.

The two parties in every option transaction are the buyer and the seller, or writer. In a typical option contract, the buyer agrees to pay or sell a certain amount of currency at a guaranteed price—called the *strike* price or *exercise* price—if the buyer chooses to.

The *principal* is the amount of currency that can be bought or sold under the contract.

Each option applies for a specific period of time before the expiration (also called *expiry*) date. In American-style options, the buyer can exercise his right to the option on any business day up to and including the day the option expires. In European-style options, the buyer has the right to exercise the option at any time, but the currency is delivered on the expiration date.

To buy an option, an investor must pay the premium. If the investor does not exercise the option, he or she loses the premium.

The premium price varies, depending on how likely the market believes the option will be exercised. For example, some premiums are simply the difference between the current spot price and the future strike price. Others use complicated formulas based mostly on current market conditions and the time before the option expires. Options are bought, sold, and resold as the market changes. Typically, however, less than 20 percent of options are actually exercised at the expiry date.

Options typically can be bought in two different settings—on an exchange or in interbank (also called over the counter [OTC], as discussed in a moment). Exchanges generally standardize their options, setting the strike price, the contract size, and the expiration date. They typically offer American-style options. Options offered on the interbank market can vary, because the buyer and seller can negotiate specific points before making a deal. These options tend to be in the European style.

The Chicago Mercantile Exchange (CME) is one of the major exchanges where currency options can be traded. It offers standardized and customized options, although primarily only in the currencies of strong economies—the U.S. dollar, the euro, the yen, the Australian dollar, the Canadian dollar, the British pound, and the Mexican peso.

Swaps

In simple terms, a *swap* is when two entities trade currency on one date and then agree to trade it back again on a specific date. In more technical terms, a swap is a combination of a spot trade and a forward.

A swap is usually used by investors who need to generate liquidity in a currency. For example, if a trader with dollars needs pounds sterling, he can swap for them. The spot transaction provides pounds, and the agreement to buy back dollars in the future gives the buyer the use of pounds until then. This is a good alternative to simply borrowing a foreign currency.

Swaps tend to be used by larger players in the Forex market, especially corporations. Individual traders typically do not use swaps.

Derivatives and the Forex Market

You may decide that one or two of the instruments just described are worth using. You also should know how other players use these instruments and how that plays out in the Forex market.

In late November 2001, I noticed that the yen had been steadily weakening against the U.S. dollar for the entire month. On the third Friday of the month, I was surprised to see the yen move in a strange fashion. It would start gaining value rapidly, and just as it appeared to break out into a higher trading value, it would suddenly fall back to lower levels.

This happened four or five times in late New York trading alone. On the charts, it looked like the yen would rise and then hit an electric fence. I had never seen anything like it. What was going on? I then heard a rumor that explained this unique event. It turned out that a Japanese importer had taken out a large put option to protect his revenue in U.S. dollars. To ensure that this option didn't expire worthless, he had enlisted a few large banks to protect his position. Whenever the yen weakened to the point of threatening his position, the banks would start selling dollars, thereby causing the yen to strengthen.

This is a pretty extreme example, but traders must understand how their trading tools interact with others. There is no doubt that the increased popularity and sophistication of financial derivatives has complicated trading, especially in price discovery. Many inexperienced Forex traders concentrate on the spot vehicle because of its relative simplicity, but this focus handicaps their ability to trade effectively.

Why? Spot is traded "over the counter" (OTC), meaning outside an organized exchange. No one can really keep track of it, because many of the trades are occurring out of sight, in different locations, and so on.

On an exchange, however, important information can be gleaned from the ebb and flow of derivative trading and posted for investors to see. The Chicago Mercantile Exchange, for example, reports outstanding positions for options. This indicates what the market thinks will happen in the future. In the fragmented, decentralized Forex spot market, however, these kinds of indicators do not exist.

A good trader knows that it's not just his investment that's important, but where he chooses to make his investment.

The Interbank Market

The Forex market functions like an international over-the-counter market. This market can be broken into two tiers—the interbank market (wholesale) and the retail market.

The Forex OTC market has no physical centralized location. The New York Stock Exchange (NYSE) has its imposing structure of pillars and marble on Wall Street. The NYSE has a trading floor of blinking lights and shouting traders. Even other exchanges or ECNs that don't have physical trading floors, such as the National Association of Securities Dealers Automatic Quotation System (NASDAQ), have a centralized network where all trade information is collected and disseminated.

But the Forex OTC is formed by disconnected players who deal directly with each other. Roughly two-thirds of all Forex transactions occur between banks, financial institutions, and central banks. This informal network of dealers and brokers is called the *interbank market*. Trading in this market is primarily based on credit and trading size, generally in the hundreds of millions. Over 200 international banks worldwide, representing every time zone, have a presence in this unique marketplace.

Because of the trade size and credit requirements, most Forex traders never get inside the interbank market. Instead, they trade in what is called the *retail* or *client* Forex market. Speculators trade with an intermediary who then moves the trades into the interbank market. This accounts for roughly 18 percent of Forex trading volume.

Since there is no centralized market, activity on the interbank market gives investors the best sense of where currencies are moving based on supply and demand.

But not all of this information gets out to investors. A true currency rate therefore can be different than what some parts of the market see. In short, there is not a single currency price at any one time. Traders must take into account large trades that occur quietly between large players on the inside.

An example is a deal between two major banks that is carried out over the phone—or "voice-brokered." Since the deal is between two self-regulating agencies in an unregulated market, the trade never has to be reported to a centralized institution or exchange. The only two players who know the new price of that particular currency can trade on the information.

Banks, however, have a view of these trades, so this gives them a major advantage over the small retail investor scanning his computer screen for news. Eventually, news of the trade gets out, but by then the banks that participated in the trade already have anticipated the move and have adjusted their investments accordingly. The retail investor is the last to know. This "flow" trading plays a critical role in price movement and this lack of transparency significantly handicaps a retail trader.

(As an aside, although trading over the computer dominates the current Forex market, phone calls still play an important role. It might seem simple, but banks still pick up the phone and call one another. There is a reason for this. Investors with unusual or large trades sometimes prefer to keep their trades on the phone, where they can be secure and private.)

This advantage, however, is not dominant. Retail investors have incredibly fast access to the Forex market because of recent developments in technology.

Technology has always been essential to the success of foreign exchange markets. The term *cable*, a trading term for the British pound, comes from the fact that decades ago a transatlantic communication wire went from Britain to the U.S. for currency traders to trade.

One of the most dramatic shifts in the Forex markets has been the rise of trading through computers, rather than the traditional order over a telephone or electronic chat. The New York Federal Reserve Bank reported in 2001 that the use of electronic trading systems—such as EBS and Reuters 3000—accounts for more than 54 percent of total interbank spot Forex trading, up from less than 33 percent in 1998.

Most of these trades are carried on two platforms: EBS and Reuters. Historically, large traders in the interbank market have always preferred Reuters. This business news organization, based in London, was among the first to establish a system that could communicate electronically with counterparties all over the world. EBS, a UK foreign-exchange solution provider launched in 1993, claims to carry orders from 2,000 traders on 750 dealing floors around the world. These two applications provided the usable technology that ushered in the Forex revolution, making the traditional phone conversation appear as modern as smoke signals.

EBS and Reuters technology harnessed the communications power of the Internet and created the only semblance of a marketplace for traders on the interbank. For the first time, traders could access the global community, which provided unprecedented liquidity and depth for spot transactions. Today, most retail platforms you will encounter have been modeled after EBS (see Figure 5.1).

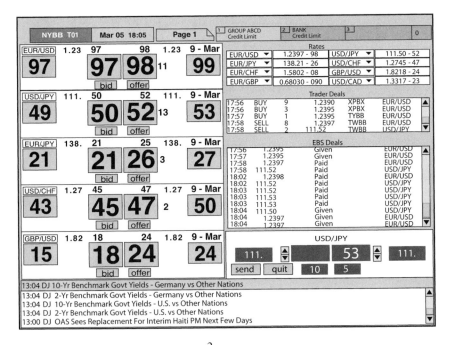

Figure 5.1– EBS spot trading screen.[2]

James H. Sinclair

James H. Sinclair is senior management with EBS Dealing Resources, Inc. In this interview, he talks about the evolution of EBS and market consolidation within foreign exchange.

I think it's fair to say that as time has gone on, transparency, as far as what the retail trader sees, is not terribly different than the interbank market, except at the most volatile times, such as when an economic announcement is issued. I have not studied pricing in the retail market in detail, so I might be wrong, but I believe it is very similar.

The key distinction between the wholesale markets, including interbank, and retail is that in the wholesale markets the minimum size is 1 million units of base currency (usually USD or EUR), whereas the retail market trades in smaller amounts. In addition, the interbank market doesn't operate in every currency pair. You have to "leg" through interbank pairs to get to many of the pairs that you see in the retail market. Most importantly, participants in the interbank market are assuming large-scale, short-term risk. I mean by short-term minutes or even seconds; they are high-frequency traders. So key distinctions include size, the number of pairs available to trade, and the time frame.

Take me through the basic evolution of EBS.

During the first year and a half, 1993 to early 1995, liquidity was patchy. One of the first currency pairs that found traction was the German Deutsche mark against the French franc (DEM/FRF). It found traction in London initially. I think one of the reasons was that DEM/FRF was a small market. After that, [it was the] USD against the mark. I remember being at a bank in

Hong Kong. The traders were looking at the EBS screen, and they were talking to their traditional voice broker. The voice broker was assuring the dealers that they were getting the best price while on the EBS screen they could see a better price.

What EBS did was to bring together all the market prices into a single place from what was a very fragmented market. So at that point, standing in that bank in Hong Kong, I could see we had a great concept.

Originally there were three electronic platforms. There was EBS, Reuters, and a Japanese broker called Minex. EBS and Minex were similar in that they were both formed by a consortium of banks plus, in the case of Minex, Japan's major broker and KDD. It wasn't too long before EBS and Minex realized that together they would compete more effectively against Reuters.

In March 1996 we merged. At that point we had a discussion about which platform to use, and in the end we decided to use EBS. This merger brought us USD/JPY. So EBS became the major broker of the first and second most actively traded spot currency pairs in the world—dollar-mark and dollar-yen.

This was what the market participants wanted. Now traders had one platform that provided liquidity for the top pairs.

The market then went through a period of growth. 1997 and 1998 were especially volatile years, primarily due to the Asian financial crisis. New events in Asia, which is the first time zone to trade, permeated through each global trading day. The years 1999 and 2000 saw the introduction of the euro, which took a significant amount of trading activity out of the market. The market lost about 30 percent of its volume. There were several reasons for that.

It was not really the loss of the pre-euro legacy currency pairs themselves but the fact that the euro had no history. So people who were technical traders had no history to go against, and those trading on fundamentals also had nothing to gauge movements on. So when an unemployment number came out in, say, France, a trader didn't know how it would affect the value of the new currency. Institutions, hedge funds, and CTAs perhaps became a little shy about what they wanted to do. [The euro introduction] was also on the back of LTCM and Y2K. Y2K made for a difficult 4Q in 1999, as many people became very risk-averse. The market has since made a very robust recovery and continued to grow.

There were some other trends that occurred at the end of the '90s. Banking consolidation took place in several forms. There were major bank mergers. Also, banks tended to trade interbank foreign exchange out of fewer centers globally. Before the late '90s most banks would, for example, each have an office in Tokyo, Hong Kong, and Singapore. In some cases, each center within the bank acted almost as an independent trading entity. Nowadays banks try to funnel their FX to one centralized location in each region and then cover the positions.

So, in the '90s if a customer were to phone a bank in Sydney, for example, to hedge a yen exposure, the bank might use EBS to cover that position in Sydney. Now the banks would send the order to a single location in each region where it might be covered. The banks often choose different locations within a region for each currency—for example, yen in Tokyo and other currencies in Hong Kong or Singapore. This trend to funnel orders through a single regional center also led to contraction and consolidation in the FX market in the late '90s.

Since 2000, the market has expanded dramatically. Just look at the BIS results: the spot interbank market expanded from $387 billion a day to $621 billion a day. There are many reasons for this. Some are macroeconomic, such as a trending dollar. Other trends are systemic and relate to the structure of the foreign exchange market, increased access, less friction in transactions, and increasing popularity of FX as an asset class.

We think there are some fundamental reasons why this market will continue to grow. For example, automation through APIs and STP. The growing trend of automation has cut down manual movements associated with each trade. With automated trading systems, since a trader doesn't have to manually hit a button, they can generate more trades. Also there is increased access to the market. FX is a credit-dependent instrument. The growth of prime brokerage has made and is making a big difference. Previously you would have to set up a credit line at every bank you wanted to trade with. With prime brokerage, you now have a facility whereby you can get your credit from one institution and your execution from another. This gives customers better access to the market. You can have a range of executing banks but only need one or two banks to get you credit.

Talk about prime brokerage and the role it plays in EBS.

In traditional foreign exchange, a customer phones a bank for execution and would have to get a credit line from that bank. Credit and execution were from the same bank. Now, with prime brokerage, customers have a variety of options. They can get execution and credit from the same bank, or they can call a bank with whom they have a trading relationship but no credit. This is sometimes called a "spoke bank" or "executing bank." They can then "give up" the trade to one or two banks with whom they have prime broker credit relationships. The single trade with the executing bank becomes two trades—one between the customer and the prime broker, and another between the prime broker and the executing bank. The net is it is easier to get your business done with a range of banks yet have a credit relationship with only one.

EBS has a service that it offers to smaller banks and similar high-frequency, large-volume trading institutions. The service, EBS Prime, functions a little differently from general prime brokerage. The customer, called an EBS Prime Customer and typically a smaller bank, comes to EBS through the eyes of a larger and very credit-strong bank, the EBS Prime Bank. The EBS Prime Customer looks at his screen and sees exactly the same prices that the EBS Prime Bank sees in the market. When the EBS Prime Customer executes a trade, it automatically becomes two trades: one between the EBS Prime Customer and the EBS Prime Bank, and another between the EBS Prime Bank and the counterparty. So now small banks have the ability to do trades, have increased access to market, and have the availability of better credit.

All of this means that when a customer is trying to execute, there is less friction entering the market and less slippage. [Slippage is the price at which the customer wanted to execute versus the price at which the trade was actually executed.] With less friction, there is increased access to the FX market and also a choice of prime brokers. We believe this will result in people being more willing to allocate additional capital to trading FX.

Have you seen a rise in investors?

Well, yes—in the FX market as a whole. With better access to the market, investors are more willing to participate in this market as an asset class in its own right.

Has technology played a role in FX development?

Absolutely. It's been very necessary to achieve the current market scale. When I talked about high-frequency dealing earlier, 500 milliseconds is a long time in foreign exchange. EBS itself is doing USD 110 billion a day on average. So the need for exact processing is critical.

FX is a self-regulated market, and EBS has played a role in defining rules within this market. Can you talk a little about that?

Well, it's important to understand that while the interbank is self-regulated, there are strict codes of conduct to which market participants subscribe. The global foreign exchange association, the ACI, publishes a Model Code. And each country has a version of that code. And EBS has its own dealing rules specifically describing how dealers and customers should use the system that incorporates the Model Code by reference.

The main rules revolve around not manipulating prices, which is enforced by the strength of the EBS system itself.

Does EBS have any thoughts on the retail market?

We hope that the retail market is very successful. Ultimately that volume flows into the interbank market through the retail customer's banking relationship. We don't see ourselves participating in the retail market directly, but we benefit, as do all market participants, indirectly. Indeed, the nature of the market is that all participants ultimately benefit from each other. The retail customer is able to get the continuous pricing that he can get only because he is part of such a huge, liquid market. The retail, corporate, institutional, and interbank participants—including brokers such as ourselves—benefit from the diversity and totality of the foreign exchange market. The market exists in its current form because the participants have each other.

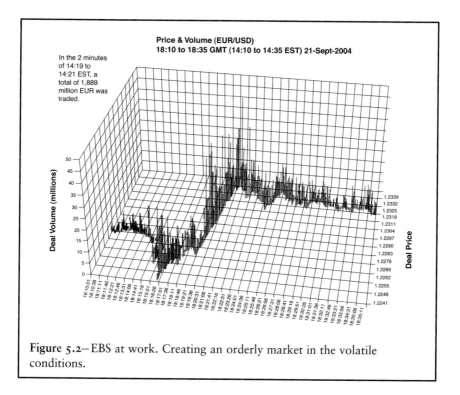

Figure 5.2—EBS at work. Creating an orderly market in the volatile conditions.

Endnotes

1. Millman, Gregory J. *The Vandal's Crown: How Rebel Currency Traders Overthrew the World's Central Banks.* New York: The Free Press, 1995.

2. Source: EBS.

6

TOOLS AND STRATEGIES TO GET STARTED

Gut Check: What It Takes to Be a Forex Investor

I was flipping through the TV channels early one Sunday, enjoying the few hours before the markets in Asia opened, when I saw an advertisement for Forex. The spot featured a "testimonial" from an "actual Forex trader." The trader was a cattle farmer in Montana or some other western state. He was standing in his pasture, talking about his experience in international investing and how Forex was the market of the future.

During the boom markets of the late '90s, I grew used to seeing commercials or stories about traders in remote or strange places, but this spot bothered me. It wasn't that the investor had begun trading or that he had become successful. What angered me was his advertised trading "strategy." He claimed that the Forex market was easy. He could wake up, place his trade, and come back later in the day to collect his gains. In between, he had time to do his chores around the farm.

If there is one thing this market is *not*, it's easy. Every Forex trader must share a worldwide market with central banks, international financial institutions, portfolio managers, and other traders. Moreover, the market's volatility makes trading a time-consuming and often exhausting experience. I have sat for 48 hours straight, watching a position dance 15 pips above my emergency sell price.

Forex is a hard market to trade—physically as well as mentally. A trader cannot simply enter a trade and then go about his or her day. I cannot stress this enough. The market does not have defined trade periods, so moves can occur anytime within a 24-hour period. This constant stress can break down a trader in a short period of time, whether he or she is winning or losing.

With this in mind, every investor, no matter where he wants to put his money, must first ask himself some hard questions. Do I understand the investment fully? Am I aware of the degree of risk? How does it fit in with my portfolio and my investment objectives? Am I prepared to invest the necessary time and energy required to make sound decisions about my investments?

Each question is important and requires an honest answer. If you can't answer these questions, you'll have better luck going to Las Vegas and playing the slot machines or investing in a less-stressful asset class, such as fixed income.

If you can't answer these questions honestly, you also will lose money. Take a cold, hard look at yourself. There is no shame in not being able to watch your investments lose value—it's a natural instinct. But successful investors know that losing money is inevitable and that keeping investing discipline is essential to achieving success.

The key is to understand your tendencies. Does the idea of losing money keep you up at night? Can you absorb financial news without becoming emotional? Do you make investment decisions quickly based on the latest trend or tip? Again, there is nothing wrong with answering yes to these questions, but you may be more comfortable with investments that are more conservative than those on the foreign exchange market.

However, even if you stay calm and focused with your investments, making money in Forex also requires active study and consistent attention to markets around the world. This means educating yourself about the Forex markets (reading this book is a good start) and checking various news outlets to keep up with changes.

Once you have thought about these questions, you should consider whether Forex trading suits your investment goals. As I've said before, Forex is an incredibly dynamic market with enormous opportunities, but it can also lead to quick losses over the short term. It should be considered a high-risk investment only suitable for those investors who can also absorb the losses that can build up as the market jumps or plunges. It is not a place to stash a retirement account or a nest egg for a home.

Personally, I recommend that a beginning investor put no more than 2 percent of his or her total assets in Forex. If you are more experienced and have had some track record of success, I would be comfortable increasing that number to 5 percent. I developed this number by looking at the benefit of having a noncorrelated commodity in every portfolio.

Once you have a good idea of your strengths and weaknesses as an investor, be aware of some dangers all investors face, no matter their style or tolerance for risk. Everyone must avoid the following common mistakes:

- **You don't have a plan**—If you can't explain why you are making a trade and what you will do if it either succeeds or doesn't, you don't have a plan. Trading "on the fly" or by instinct leads to losses. Hope is not a plan. The second half of this tip is to be disciplined with your plan. Once you've picked a strategy, stick with it. Don't improvise, or you won't learn from your mistakes.

- **You trade against the market**—Many investors think they know something the markets don't. When an investment slides, they hang in there. When it falls further, they simply buy more, convinced that the market will rebound and they will reclaim their losses. This can happen, but not often enough to form the basis of a strategy. Catching a reversal is a very difficult strategy. Don't become so attached to your position that you lose sense of objective market forces. When a position turns sour, cut your losses. The other half of this tip is don't sell a profitable position until it hits your target. If you have thought through your plan, you will end up with far more profits than losses.

What Are My Investment Goals, and Are They Realistic?

I often think Forex today resembles California more than 150 years ago during the gold rush. There are expectations of enormous returns, and marketers are happy to encourage this. As during the gold rush, enormous profits have been made in the Forex market.

And it's easy to see how more can be made. Without doing any real research and simply by looking at any currency chart, a trader can see that being on the right side of a move, while heavily leveraged, can make a small bet pay off well.

There is no denying those charts, and we all have heard the stories of speculators, such as George Soros, raking in $3 billion in three days of trading. As with any market, somewhere between the myths and facts lies the truth. Forex is no different. There is a lot of money to be made, but the risks are real. Investors must understand this before developing a trading strategy. Forex, even with its wild volatility, is still tied to the general rules of returns. Just because Forex is the largest market in the world doesn't mean we should suspend reality. "Risk versus reward" is still relevant. You can't put down $20,000, leverage it 100 to 1, and expect to retire on your returns. Always remember that great money managers look for 15- to 20-percent returns over the long term. Most sweat just to beat the major indexes.

What Is My Capacity for Risk?

The Forex market reflects the global environment. Just by turning on CNN you can see how unpredictable things really are. In autumn 2004, two unrelated factors pulled the U.S. dollar lower—hurricanes in Florida and a strike on the oil pipelines in Nigeria. The price of oil soared above $53 a barrel. No analyst can forecast what are essentially random events.

In comparison, share prices of blue-chip stocks with constant, predictable cash flow, such as McDonalds and Coca-Cola, hardly fluctuate on a daily basis. They can show dramatic movements over time, and they can spike after announcements, earnings reports, or analyst meetings. Compared to Forex, however, they are stable. For example, a recent memo by a major Forex firm effectively said that recent market conditions had caused "temporary illiquidity." Consequently, the Forex market could drop or gain 100 to 200 pips in a matter of minutes. In response, they couldn't guarantee execution for stop-loss, limit, and entry orders. If you had a stop-loss order at 122.00 EUR/USD and something unexpected happened that caused the U.S. dollar to suddenly and violently strengthen, the market might skip your order and execute at the next available price—maybe 121.

As with any margin account, the investor is responsible for all losses. This introduces a whole new level of risk to the average investor, because set risk levels protected by stop-loss orders can be nullified in extreme cases. And since a currency can't be worth zero, there is no bottom.

Time Investment

As we've discussed before, the Forex market reacts to events occurring all over the world, and rarely do events occur in an orderly fashion. I have often sat in front on my terminal having a silent conversation—"OK, I'm ready to trade. Now, market, move." Or I might think, "If this currency breaks this resistance, I will place an order." Then I wait 10 hours for London to open for the event to finally occur.

Investors must understand that just because they have set aside a few hours to watch the market in anticipation of a trade doesn't mean the market will provide an opportunity.

A great example is from 2002, when President Bush was preparing to invade Iraq. The troops were in place and the president had publicized his intent to the world. The only real question was when. On March 20, 2003 the U.S. launched cruise missiles into Baghdad around 9 p.m. EST, two hours before the UN deadline. New York was getting ready for bed, and Japan was heading to work. Considering the huge movements that had already occurred in the markets in anticipation of the attack, the market reaction when the bombs finally started falling was slight. However, it illustrates the commitment and dedication an investor needs in this market. Even if you trade purely on technical grounds, the volatility of this market demands attention and constant reevaluation. It is very difficult to be a part-time trader; I advise against it.

Before You Trade

The Forex markets are different from markets you may already be familiar with, and that can require a different perspective and trading strategy. In 2005, Rick Santelli, a respected commentator on the Chicago Mercantile Exchange, once said, "This bond market is not your dad's bond market," referring to unique changes in fixed-incomes trading behavior. Santelli's comment can just as easily be applied to the Forex market.

If you know stock markets very well in the U.S., you may be aware of their rhythms. This refers to the rises and dips in trading activity from 9:30 a.m. to 4 p.m. EST. Some of these changes in activity are based on human behavior. Just before most traders go to lunch, there tends to be a noticeable rise in trading volume as they squeeze in trades before they take their break.

The Forex market also displays these kinds of patterns, but over a 24-hour time period. Trading, for example, tends to pick up at certain times that correspond to the trading schedules of different cities. For example, trading always gets brisk around 4 a.m. EST, when London opens. It sags again at 11 p.m., when Tokyo closes and before London opens. It jumps when New York opens and just before London closes.

Crossing Over to the Forex Market

In an interview, Barry Calder of Hotspot FX, one of the original retail Internet Forex trading firms, discussed the kinds of traders who were using his product to trade Forex. Many of them are traders who are already comfortable trading equities.

"We are finding clients from the equity side, with day-trading experience, and we absorb this quite well. There is not that much involved with Forex. It's basically buying and selling, rates moving up and down, and it's very easy to calculate the P/L, price of pips and fees involved, and now it's all automated. Depending on how much expertise these traders have and how successful they have been in the equity markets, we suggest they do as much reading as possible on the individual instruments since each trade is different. Euro/USD and USD? Yen will trade very differently than the pattern of trading on an IBM or Microsoft. Those traders with a true trading mentality do not have a difficult time adjusting and crossing over into the Forex world. But there is a difference between trading and traditional investing. The people that are successful in Forex have a definite strategy and stick to it. It's not necessarily the time frame but the mentality. Those traders that are not doing well tend to be undereducated or not sticking to their disciplines."

Doing a Test Run

A good method to learn how the Forex market works is to take a practice run before you do the real thing. Fortunately, many retail platforms offer investors the chance to trade a simulated account for several months. You can use this opportunity to develop a trading strategy, become accustomed to new market conditions and movements, and learn how the platform works. (A list of major Forex firms that offer demo accounts is provided in Chapter 8, "Inside a Forex Platform," in the sidebar titled, "Forex Trading Platforms.") An investor should always take a practice run with any platform before trading with real funds, regardless of his or her experience.

The concept that the season is made in the preseason is true. The more real you make your "paper" trades, the better equipped you will be to handle real market conditions. Mistakes are common when the adrenaline is pumping during a heated trade. And calling your FCM to say "I made a mistake" will not be taken lightly. Rarely does the FCM change a trade.

The key to making this trial run successful is to execute plans rather than just trades. Keep a careful log of your moves and what strategy you are following. Make all your mistakes "profitable" by learning what went wrong and why, and how you can prevent it from happening again.

Strategy: Creating an Approach Model

Every trader needs to develop his or her own approach to the Forex market—one that is both successful and a match between the trader's personality and trading behavior. A good match between the trader and his approach will be more profitable and will allow the trader to locate flaws quickly and make adjustments. The size and scope of the Forex market can make developing an approach intimating for most traders. Where do you begin?

A classic model is the inverted pyramid approach, shown in Figure 6.1. In this model you can pinpoint trades while evaluating all the risks associated with them. Most brokers, traders, and dealers follow this model—consciously or just instinctively.

The basic approach is to select a currency pair to trade. Then consider all the trade's macroeconomic factors at the top of the inverted pyramid. As you go down the pyramid, list technical considerations until you get to the tip. The pyramid should show the trader all the factors related to a trade. Depending on his or her style, the trader can weight the pyramid accordingly. Fundamental traders, for example, stay on the top portion of the pyramid, weighting it 100%, and pure technical traders inhabit the bottom.

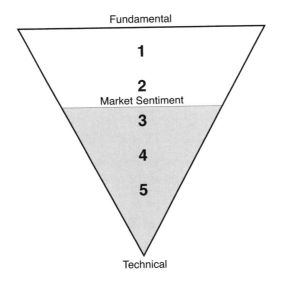

Figure 6.1—The inverted pyramid model.

Here is how a trader uses the inverted pyramid model:

   1. **Macro overview**—This is a broad look at the overriding feeling of the world. What is the world facing? Is it global terrorism, SARS, impending war, oil prices, or the Christmas shopping season? Is the mood optimistic or pessimistic? The best way to gauge this is to watch any credible 24-hour news station, such as CNN or BBC.

2. **Market specifics**—This is where you review the actual currency markets. What are the markets looking at? If it's important, every analyst will be talking about it. Is it a G7 meeting, a central bank rate meeting, the latest comments from Alan Greenspan, or a major move in another asset class that could affect currencies? For example, suppose you are considering selling U.S. dollars and buying Swiss francs because you are worried about global uncertainty. Then you discover that the Swiss population is about to vote on a referendum to join the euro. Perhaps waiting for the referendum risk to dissipate would be smarter.

   Market sentiment—At this point, a trader should get a strong handle on the overall market sentiment. The *market sentiment* is the general feeling surrounding the currency market. This behavior indicator is critical in developing a smart trade. Is the market looking for a big move? Is the market confused regarding what direction it should be heading toward? The easiest way to gauge market sentiment is to read analyst reports and watch live news channels. Eventually, you will be able to piece together a complete picture of the market.

3. **Indicators and price changes**—Now that you have a good understanding of the known macro environment, you should have an idea of currency pairs that will be volatile. These are the currency pairs you should focus on. (With a world of economic indicators, monitoring everything is impossible.) What are the important indicators, and what are non-events? Each indicator affects markets differently. The key to filtering out the noise is a solid grasp of the macro environment. Also consider the recent movement of prices. Is there a clear trend or spiky volatility?

At this point you should focus on the potential for a trade. By considering the three factors just listed, you should be able to narrow down the most probable currency pairs. At the next stage of the process, technical considerations offer the best way to define trading points:

4. **Basic technicals (support and resistance)**—Whether or not you rely on technicals, you should realize that technical "floors" and "ceilings" have become valid psychological trading levels. Any veteran in the market will tell you that traders sit on those levels. By watching technical patterns, you can begin to formulate a view on a specific currency pair's directional movement.

   Specific currency market sentiment—Once a currency pair is chosen, its unique market sentiment should be reviewed.

5. **Micro indicators**—This is the fine-tuning of a strategy by defining actual entry and exit points before a trade is executed. Each trader must find the technical indicator that is effective for his or her strategy. Some like stochastic indicators (involving chance or randomness); others prefer weighting moving averages.

Here's a real-life example of using the inverted pyramid strategy:

Wednesday, December 1, 2004

- **Step 1**—At 5:30 a.m. New York time, a scan of the BBC shows that the world is relatively quiet, warily waiting for the holidays. News on Iraq and the war on terrorism is being played down, and President Bush is visiting Canada. Ukraine is showing political instability after its election, but the risk of anything truly affecting the global marketplace is limited, so it's not worth reviewing.

- **Step 2**—The biggest news is about the U.S. dollar and its decline against other major currencies, especially the euro. The day before, the USD/EUR went to new all-time highs—reaching the 1.333 area. The huge current U.S. account deficit, exacerbated by Congress's recent passing of $800 billion in new debt, combined with a war that is not progressing, have fueled already-rabid speculation against the U.S. dollar. The ECB's Trichet calls the euro's rise "brutal," but the market is unconvinced that this verbal intervention will lead to any effective action. The dollar market is clearly in a negative environment, and the way it disregards higher-than-expected U.S. Q3 GDP numbers tells me that normal indicators will not reverse this downward trend.

- **Step 3**

    Economic and Monetary Union (EMU)
    10.00 PMI Manufacturing (Nov)
    11.00 GDP (Q3) Q/Q Y/Y
    11.00 Unemployment Rate (Oct)

    U.S.
    14.30 Personal Income (Oct) M/M
    14.30 Personal Spending (Oct) M/M
    14.30 PCE Deflator (Oct) Y/Y
    14.30 PCE Core Deflator (Oct) Y/Y
    16.00 Construction Spending (Oct)
    16.00 ISM Manufacturing (Nov)
    16.00 ISM Prices Paid (Nov)
    16.30 DOE U.S. Crude Oil Inventories (Nov 26)
    16.30 DOE U.S. Gasoline Inventories
    20.00 Fed's Beige Book
    Domestic Vehicle Sales (Nov)

Events
11.00 European Commission 4th Qtr and 1st Qtr GDP Forecast
18.30 BOE King speaks
20.10 Fed's Yellen speaks on U.S. economic outlook

Step 4—The trading environment from the days before allows me to rule out any real market impact from the list of indicators. Even the meeting with Fed governor Yellen, or the release of the Fed's beige book, which normally would have market impact, won't stop the dollar's slide this time.

Step 5—Considering the market from a technical viewpoint, I see that support is around 1.3230, which it hit two days in a row and bounced right up. Resistance is seen at 1.3330, the day's high. It is also the all-time high for EUR/USD. This is a major point of resistance. There is a good probability that if either of these numbers breaks, the currency will move sharply in that direction.

Given the complete picture, this setup has the makings of a strong USD decline; a really simple play would be a buy EUR/USD above the resistence at 1.3330. Stops and limits should be pre-defined by your overall trading strategy.

7

FOREX FROM THE
INSIDE

In this chapter, participants in Forex—from multinational corporations to international banks, to FCM dealers, to retail traders—describe their roles in the currency markets.

Joachim Herr
Joachim Herr is the head of risk management at BMW International. In this interview, he discusses how BMW handles currency exposure and trading methodologies.

Whenever we sell a car—for example, in Thailand—we get Thai baht (THB), but our cost basis is to a large extent in euros. What we need to make sure of from a currency perspective is that the THB revenue we receive is worth more than our euro-denominated costs in order to stay comfortable. Without risk management, the large exchange rate fluctuations would lead to times of very high profitability (when the THB is strong) and times of low profitability (when the THB is weak). To ensure that this does not happen is the goal of risk management here at BMW Group. We make sure that the fluctuations of the currency do not impact our operating business, which is producing and selling cars. Therefore, the first thing we do on a weekly basis is review our risk positions. This is the most critical thing in currency management—know what your risk is. So we look at monthly, yearly, and 7-year-long ranges. We look at what the expected sales are—for example, in THB—and the currency flows that are involved so we know what our risk positions are. For the second step, I look at the currency market and the state of currencies. We have developed an internal model of the currency movements for a very long time since we have been using this model, which gives us a sort of long-term fair value of the foreign currency. It is derived from things like purchasing power parity (PPP), trend following models. What we have seen is that in the short term the exchange rates can deviate quite significantly from the fair value in both directions, but in the long run we see a mean reversion tendency. So the next step is we look at the THB in comparison to the euro right now compared to our fair-value analysis. If the THB is currently very strong, then we say, "Yes, that is a good opportunity for us to lock in that very favorable exchange rate for a long time." Then we enter long-term hedge contracts to make sure for a very long time that the cars that we sell in

Thailand are very profitable. In times when the TBH is underval-ued, we do not enter into long-term contracts but only short-term expirations to make sure in 3 to 6 months we don't have currency risks. But we would stay away from, say, 3- or 4-year contracts. The effect of this is on the one hand we eliminate short-term fluc-tuations by short-term risk measures, and in the long run we make sure we have a sort of smoothing of the exchange rate that we achieve. In the long run we don't let the currency fluctuations affect the operational business of BMW.

Does BMW stay away from specific currencies, such as liquid or emerging?

Yes, it happens, but these are in the less-developed countries. Most of the markets that we operate in have a higher degree of development. In the less-developed countries there is often no substantial market for BMW Group products. So we usually work in countries with a little bit more development. Usually it goes along with developed currency markets. While these coun-tries don't have such liquidity as, say, the U.S. dollar, we can still do something. And whenever we find a currency market with significant market participants, we try to adapt our model of long-term currency price hedging to this market as well.

How actively do you trade in the FX markets?

I'm reluctant to talk about trading because I don't see myself as a trader. A trader, in my view, is always trading both ways—selling and buying and trying to make a profit on it. That's not our goal. What we see ourselves as is hedgers, and what we do is for the very long term, hedges in a 4-to-5-year time frame, and this is not done on an hourly basis. So we analyze the currency very carefully. For example, in 2001 we saw a very large overvaluation of the U.S. dollar, so we entered into long-term hedging contracts.

When it comes to short-term operational transitions or technical hedging, we make sure that currency volatility does not impact us in the next 3 months. I'm in the market for these shorter-term, smaller-scale transitions every day. But only on one side: selling the foreign currency.

What about BMW trading mechanisms?

Yes, we have five active traders worldwide. I have two on my team in Munich who do FX and commodities, two in New York for the USD area, and one in the UK for pound trades. In all other countries, because we have different approaches for the execution of the trade, the local treasurer has the responsibility. So, for example, the treasurer of BMW Thailand, as part of the job in the front office, regulates the local currency exposure. For the normal treasurer it takes about 10 percent of work time.

How does BMW transact its FX transitions?

We are allowed to use any electronic platform and all instruments available to us. Currently I would say we do about 90 percent of our trades over the phones, directly with the banks, and roughly 5 percent via trading platforms but closed trading systems. For example, we use the UBS system. We are currently not using any open systems like FX at all because all of these platforms, as good as they may be, have restrictions on the back part. We would only consider changing if it was a truly open system to all banks. That is better handled over the phone, since if you need a four-year forward you get a better price than an electronic system.

Take me through a trade.

There are two scenarios one must consider. Let's look at the USD. First is the USD overvaluation, and the other is the USD undervaluation. In the first scenario of the USD overvaluation, if the USD is overvalued at .90, like it was in 2001, I look at my model in the morning and say, "Oops, the USD is at .90." Let's see. My risk position is 1 billion USD over the next few years, and I still have 50 percent open for 2008. The USD is favorable, so I want to close the position in 2008. When I decide in the weekly currency counsel, I call up the bank and I trade directly with the bank, 300m 50 September 2008. And that is a very long-term transaction and strategy. That type of transaction is not fit for a normal trade floor because of infrequency of trades. These trades are carefully studied and thought about.

There are times like in 1997 when the market becomes more dynamic. How do you adjust? That's case number two. If we are in the overvaluation of a currency, we are in a relaxed mood. Everything is working better than we have expected or forecasted. We are relaxed. But whenever the foreign currency is undervalued, like the USD right now [June 2004], you have a different situation. Obviously, if the USD is undervalued, you don't enter into long-term future hedges. I don't come in in the morning saying, "Let's think about 2008," because at current USD rates, I wouldn't do any hedging for 2008. But I might have some open volume for next month [July]. Because whenever we hedge, we don't do 100 percent of the exposure or monthly risk. If you have a high level of certainty, you might do 90 to 95 percent. But still there is always a little open volume left. Like today [June 16, 2004], when I came in, we heard the rumors about the outlook for the CPI data, and we think about how that will affect the USD, which is a very short-term discussion. We look at technical charts, checking on whether the U.S. dollar is breaking a certain barrier or if inflation data is coming out on the higher end, because then the dollar will probably get stronger through the day. So let's not do the hedging of the June contracts this morning [German time], but wait for the CPI data in New York.

This is a typical short-term trade where market timing becomes very important.

In a nutshell, we have long-term strategic hedging, where we do very long, deep analysis on currency movements, and we have short-term technical hedging, where we decide how to cover the remaining open risk in the coming months, which is much more trading-oriented and where we look at technical charts rather than fundamentals.

What is your outlook for the U.S. dollar?

We don't have any outlook on the USD, since it is our view that the currency markets are a "random walk," and you never know where the next movement will be—the next hour or the next day. You might get a small advantage with technicals, but in the long run PPP tends to hold true. Currency reverts to PPP in the long run. In the medium run—say, 1 month to 3 years—we have no indication whatsoever. What I am sure of is in the long run we will revert to numbers around 1.10, which is in our mind fair value. Whether that happens in the next year or in 2006, I don't know. I know that our company has a conservative long-term approach to currency hedging. We are very well prepared. And our trading approach is structured so that even if the USD stays weak for the next year or so, we are relaxed since we are not gambling on currency. We manage our currency risk and exposure diligently and have done so for the last 10 years quite well to make sure our company can do what it does best—producing the best driving machine.

Steve Nutland

Steve Nutland is director of trading in North America for spot and emerging markets at Bank of America. In this interview, he talks about the role his bank plays in the Forex market, as well as some advice he learned when he first started trading.

Let's start by having you tell me a little about Bank of America and your role there.

Bank of America has been a major player in the Forex market for a number of years. We have a centralized trading focus, with our main hubs in New York, Singapore, and London. Our sales force is more satellite-focused—like Los Angeles, San Francisco, Charlotte, Chicago, Boston, Toronto, and, of course, New York. We cover all the risk centrally but handle the sales locally in the field with the client, so we can deal with our client personally. From a trading point of view, I consider the role of myself and my traders to be an advisory and execution and service-providing institution—meaning we make prices and take orders, watch orders, execute on behalf of clients.

A big part of our job is risk transference. A client, whether he is an institutional or corporate client, has an exposure. My job is to step up and take the risk where he doesn't want it. It's a tremendous amount of service provision. And then there is the advisory portion, risk-taking portion, and proprietary trading based on a combination of factors, including fundamentals and flow technicals. Some traders trade from a gut feeling and some traders trade from a more defined set of parameters. We try to have, in terms of my team, a niche which includes both proprietary traders and market makers—a good mix of both trading style and risk appetites—and we cover currencies, not only including the G10 but Asia, Latin America, Eastern Europe, and Africa.

What do you think your volume is on a daily basis?

It's in the region of $100 billion year-to-date daily turnover. A vast majority of that is considered interbank turnover. This is traders via other counterparties through interbank methods, including EBS platform and Reuters dealing platforms and a variety of other means of dealing, which still include calling out on Reuters once in a while and dealing with voice brokers. $20 billion comes from corporate business. Included in that is some of the business we transact over the platforms, such as FXall, Currenex, and all the other varieties of platforms. This includes our own platform, called fxtransaction, which is a big area for us since we are about to launch our latest streaming-rate capabilities. Instead of us using "price on request," we will now be providing a direct price with updates every tick the market makes.

Who would I see on the Bank of America Forex desk?

Historically traders have focused on specific currency pairs by looking after a specific currency. We would have had a desk of up to 50 traders with dealing assistants and other support staff. As markets have evolved and technology has changed the process, the need to have so many traders has vanished. On the spot G10 desk would be six senior traders and six junior traders. There is still a currency specialization. Traders are individually tasked with market-making certain currency pairs, so I will have a trader whose job is to call euro/USD prices. He is not limited to the risk he takes in just euros. He is not necessarily tied to only that currency pair and in fact can trade other currency pairs and products around that. So our specialization has evolved—from a "jack of all trades" to hopefully "master of more than none." Even if you were a euro/USD trader, I wouldn't be surprised to see you have risk in seven to eight other pairs as well.

What is the role of a broker in Bank of America?

A broker in the past has been one of the major sources of liquidity for spot traders. If I had a need or an interest to buy euros at a certain price, I may go to a broker and show him "I'm 40 bid 5 million euros." Hopefully that will be enough for someone who has an opposite interest to say, "I'm 40 offered 5 million euros."

Therefore, the broker has a market in euros. That was the prime market for all currency pairs, probably as long ago as 10 years. At that time, by 1994, the EBS platform was launched as a competitor to Reuters, and over the past several years it has come to dominate our marketplace. The voice broker is still in existence, and they still do a decent amount of business in the auction market, but there is an increasing number of electronic platforms in the emerging market business. The option market is predominantly done through the voice broker and in the emerging markets, short-term interest rates trading market, and even in the futures market. But in spot G10 Forex, the profile of a broker has declined to probably less than 1 percent of our volume. They are still a very useful mechanism for us and other institutions for price on request. And we would be very interested in making markets for voice brokers. When perhaps a small- or medium-tier institution has an interest in an amount he is not comfortable with clearing on the electronic platform, he may ask a voice broker for a price, and we would willingly quote them. And on occasion we will use them ourselves. But their ability to show running rates is limited, so therefore they have a hard time competing.

What's your average day at Bank of America?

I get into the office at 6:30 a.m. [EST] after probably receiving a few calls during the night. Depending on the amount of risk I have at the end of the New York day, I would speak with my London office as soon as I got into the office to get a quick rundown of what closed in the market, what orders we have seen, and go through the market—how their day was and a quick refresher course on where we are and where we are going. We have a morning meeting globally around 7 a.m. that encompasses strategies and economists' views on the market, including both fundamentals and technical, and then we go through the various trading desks and sales desks, commenting on both our ideas for the day, our risk profile, and any upcoming news and economic data that we expect to see that day. Obviously we never start the day from zero; we have positions in the market on a 24-hour basis. The Forex market, as you know, opens in Wellington around noon Sunday and closes when we close in New York Friday afternoon. That means five and a half days of trading sessions, and we are committed to being involved all the time.

I'm getting off the point, but many people believe Forex is a necessary evil. On the institutional/hedge fund side of the business, many view it as the largest casino in the world. I like to see it that somewhere in between the two lies the truth. We are happy to be involved in the 24-hour market since there is lots of money to be made, and also we have risk that's not based on the normal trading day.

Beginning at 6:30, typically there tends to be a lull in the market when New York begins the day. And our New York market really picks up speed somewhere between 8 and 8:30 a.m. Often economic data is released at 8:30—payrolls, trade balance for the U.S., for example. The majority of our trading in terms of volume is done between 8 and 12 New York time. That's the largest period of overlap, when North America and all of Europe and London are trading. There are obviously days when the market is more aggressive or active in other time periods. At 12 o'clock in New York, it's 5 in London. We often see some erratic moves as London and Europe go home and people square out their positions. And New York afternoons can vary between very skittish—where the market is really active but the liquidity is not there because Europe and Asia are home—to very dull and dreary, where we just trade and watch the hours before we go home and Asia comes to work. We pass our orders at 5:30 p.m. [EST] to our Singapore office, and our Singapore office is staffed until the London office opens. We do this to make our client experience virtually seamless. I know there have been times when I have worked a client's order on a 24-hour basis—though there is no reason why they couldn't have been passed along. We truly view Forex as a global business.

Can you take me through a risk transfer from a multinational corporation through Bank of America to a counterparty?

A few weeks ago we had a multinational corporate client who needed to hedge some exposure for the next 12 months somewhere in the range of $400 million against predominantly euros. The client released this as a relatively large amount. And if they were just to sit on that trade, there could be some substantial slippage. Some of our clients speak to more than one bank. Some clients might choose to call four banks in 100s and deal with them all at once, although that tends to have an adverse effect on the price and execution. Some client would put a hard level and say, "Can you sell them for me here?" and we would certainly do so. But if you just show your hand to the market on one of the electronic platforms, the market tends to run away from a sizable order. So we told the client that we will show them a very competitive price in the full amount and they can come in as long as the price is satisfactory. To them, they can wash their hands and eliminate their exposure, and Bank of America will take on their risk. It does open us to some downside risk, but obviously we feel there is more upside potential. And we might do one of a few things with that trade. First of all, if we like the position, we might just choose to sit on the position for a period of time. If the market moves in our favor, we might choose to exit a piece of [the position] and hold some. Or if we really do like the position, we might choose to exit the whole position. And in addition add some more euros to the trade or said currency pair, knowing that both the supply and demand in the market in the short term will have an effect in our favor and we have gotten out of a position we didn't like.

We have several means of execution. We obviously have a group of people, and since Bank of America is such a large institution, each has a different view on the market. Quite often there is risk sharing between my traders. In a trade of $400 million, we might find five or six guys will each take a piece. And we have a number of clients that we work closely with that might have an appetite for euros, so we can obviously go to them in a mutually beneficial way since they are getting euros at a level that suits them and we pass on euros we have. And really $400 million sounds like a sizable trade, but not really for Bank of America. In the course of the day that is really not that much of a position. While it might move the market for the short term—half hour or one hour—in the long term it won't. For us, we would think about sitting on a piece of the trade, or more often than not, we would not execute the whole trade. The market would smell the trade, and you wouldn't get the most economic price for the order. Our job and experience hopefully will tell us to take our time and work our way out of the position.

What are some of the tools you use?

EBS and Reuters are the predominate sources of liquidity. In New York there are any number of risk takers, and in London as well. We like to know what every other trader at Bank of America is doing at all times. There are times when I'm looking to do 100 million euros, and a Bank of America trader might say he can do the whole lot. So it's important for traders to have great communication and to maximize efficiencies and not to cross too many bid-ask spreads.

Where do you get your information?

Different traders focus on different things. We have a variety of traders who all have the standard Reuters, Dow Jones news wire on the bottom of our EBS screens. Reuters has its own news service. We take Dow Jones news—market news. Most traders have a Bloomberg terminal. Besides that, we are inundated with news wires coming into our desk. Not everyone takes everything into account, including our own in-house reports. There are tons to choose from, but outside the standard it depends on the individual trader. Both Reuters and Bloomberg have excellent charting packages included. CQG is a good stand-alone charting package. Again, it depends on the trader—if they are technical, fundamental, or a mix of both. Some traders are pure market makers, and they don't take risk for the sake of taking risk. They wait for the business to come to them. We make sure that we always have a nice blend.

How well does the retail market reflect the interbank market?

I would say less accurate. Because obviously they are not dealing with the people we are dealing with—which is classified as the professional market. If I could backtrack briefly, I would say we obviously speak with many different clients and types. And we are a major institution on the street. Our corporate clients can be very large in size, but in terms of direction for the market, it is not necessarily all that significant. It tends to be of a hedging nature rather than a directional indicator or a risk taker. Institutional business would be the global bond or equity funds, which are dealing with foreign exchange because they have to or they like to treat Forex as a separate asset class. And certainly our hedge fund and CTA clients who obviously view Forex as a separate asset class are obviously dealing in currencies, because they believe that they are going to make money in a directional trade. For us those clients are the most interesting when we are dealing with other banks that are dealing on behalf of their clients. I would argue that since the interbank market is dealing with professionals, their directional views are more relevant to us and the market in the short term. From a retail point of view, depending on your parameter and reason for trading, a guy long and a guy short can both make money. A funny anecdote: A friend of mine was trading for a major bank in Tokyo. When he went home, he reported he was square. When he came in the next morning, they have lost three-fourths of a million dollars. One guy was 50 m long and the other 50 m short, and they both had been stopped out overnight. So it can happen where both can be right and wrong, depending on your risk and time horizon. So anyone can be right. I tend to focus more on the fundamental and flow-driven side of the market. I'm not particularly focused on technical, although there are those that feel that side of the market is a self-fulfilling prophecy. Others will tell you that over the long term there are some very beneficial rewards. And there are many companies who have built whole empires on technical and systematic trading. I think at the very least you can't afford to ignore either side of the market, technical or fundamental.

If you were writing a book to the retail trader, what would have to be in that book?

I was given many tips over the years growing up as a young trader in London that I have tried to adhere to—but not always well.

Be selective with your trades. For many traders, the hardest factor to understand is to know when they are wrong. It's very easy to be right, but it is more difficult to understand when you're wrong and take appropriate action. That might not be just to exit a position but to cut and reverse the other way.

One very experienced trader told me when I was early in the market, "Never get too greedy, and always leave something on the table for someone else." I have found that to be very valuable over the years. You should not necessarily look to hit home runs every time you trade. Another key for any trader is to always know your positions. More importantly than being long where you are, but just the fact you are long. Because the Forex markets are moving all the time. Any level of a position is arguably less important than just understanding your risk and rationale for the trade. Appreciate how to manage the position.

Straightforward discipline, and at the end of the day don't get too complicated, because it's a very simple product once you understand the jargon that goes with it. You have two currencies that go up and down. So if you can trade around some strict strategies' risk exposure, sticking to your stop losses, understanding your downside as well as your upside, you should be fine.

Tim K.

Tim K. is a senior global dealer at Forex Capital Markets/Refco FX. In this interview, he discusses specific aspects of the Forex markets, including whether the retail market offers the same prices as the interbank market.

During normal market conditions, [the retail market] is spot on. The only time the price differs is during extreme volatility. This is a phenomenon that you will find occurs globally. During these extreme conditions, dealers all over the world are scrambling to fill orders and maintain some stability to be able to make a fair and orderly market. At the same time, they must protect themselves by limiting risk so they don't get run over. In extremely volatile situations, no one knows where the actual market is because traders post bids and offers very wide.

At our firm we make a fixed pip price under any market condition. This is a very difficult task when the rest of the world is making very wide prices. Fortunately, our dealers are aggressive enough to make our customers a price under any market condition. Again, I must stress, events that cause extreme volatility are rare.

What do you think are some of the pitfalls of being a retail Forex trader?

The amount of information that actually needs to be accessed by a beginner trader can be overwhelming. Once they learn to filter all the noise, then the pros outweigh the cons versus any other market. In addition, the fact that Forex is a 24-hour market, a trader needs to stay on top of all new information, fundamentals and technical, if they have an open position.

What advice would you give to new traders?

Watch the market like a hawk! Constantly assess it. This may become tiring, boring, and mentally draining, but over time you will begin to see patterns develop. Technical levels develop. Then you will find levels within those levels. In a range trading market, there will be a lot of opportunities. It is equally important to realize how all markets affect each other. For example, the dollar has a correlation to gold and oil. Oil has a correlation to the stock market. Interest rates are correlated with fixed income and, in turn, the dollar. After years of watching markets, you begin to see a pattern of smart money flowing in one market and out of the other. It's a never-ending cycle.

As a dealer, do you see any patterns in the market?

Yes. When the market is approaching key technical levels, you see a lot of buyers and sellers hovering. When the market is quiet—for example, during summertime and holidays—and there is not much going on, trading ranges develop. A savvy trader will be able to recognize patterns quickly. If you can find a trading range, you really can take advantage of that.

Tell me a story.

One of the most interesting periods in recent years was when the Bank of Japan was intervening in 2002. The USD/JPY trade was around the 120–125 level and went all the way to above 133. The BOJ would intervene several times a week. The desk would prepare for it, but you can never be fully prepared for that type of volume flooding the market. The immense volume kept pushing and pushing the dollar higher and higher. Then traders would just come in and start selling, looking for some sort of retracement. The volatility was extreme. Obviously when a currency pair goes up 200–300 pips during the Asian-European session, there is going to be some retracement. As dealers we must be prepared for this type of action every day.

Pier L.

Pier L. graduated from Syracuse University with a degree in design. She went into finance with no specific background in the field, starting as a trader's clerk in London. Soon, she was determined to trade on her own. She was told, "Girls really don't trade." She answered, "Yeah, right," and started trading on her lunch break. Eventually, she moved to another company and started trading full-time. After the September 11 attacks, she moved back to the U.S. and is today trading from her home north of New York City.

I trade out of my house. I have an office, my charts, my T1 lines, DSL lines, and my Bloomberg, and off I go. It is so funny how rapidly technology and these markets have changed in such a short period of time. I mean, I had to work in Germany because you couldn't get the connection to the exchange unless you were across the street from the exchange. Now I am in New York!

I believe in simplicity. I use CQG for my charts, Trading Technologies as my trading platform. I have used terminals such as Bloomberg and Reuters. They're great. They are wonderful, but I keep it really simple. I don't do anything too flashy for my technical analysis. I do have market numbers. I subscribe to a service as well as doing my own. Then I compare them both, and it paints a lovely market picture for me. As I mentioned earlier, I have an art background—and because of that, I think I was able to read charts so quickly because I am able to see patterns in them. Artists are also good at using the other side of their brain. I never went through a training program with my company when I started trading. They didn't really have them then. Now pretty much everyone has them.

What do you study when you consider a market?

I feel that all of these markets are like a domino effect. If A makes B tick and C tick, then watch out, D, F, and G. They will all influence each other. Asian markets, European markets, American markets, earnings, weightings, economic data, stocks, etc.

It's like a circle for me—they all influence the trade, whether it is in Europe or America.

You're up at 3 every morning. Walk me through your day.

The greatest thing for me is working from home. It allows me to really focus on what is going on in the world all the time without having to always be in an office. I don't need to go in and trade the Intel earnings, or wait to see how the market is impacted for whatever event. I am able to do it as I please.

I mainly work European hours, in terms of actually trading. I am up just before the European opening, and I am figuring out what is going on in the financial world—what Asia is doing, what New York did, looking at what data or earnings are coming out. I always have Bloomberg on, as well as a news source that comes over my CQG. I usually do my levels the night before. I watch the open and what is going on, depending on overnight news. You can have staggering openings. Between 3 and 4 a.m. you have different markets in Europe opening. Depending on the markets, I may just sit there, or trade. If it is really dead, I will take a nap for an hour, wake up, make breakfast, coffee, and trade. I have traded in Europe long enough to understand the market patterns. So going on that, I will trade the auctions at about 7 a.m. [EST]. And then most of America is waking up and the Bonds open at 8:30, then New York opens at 9:30. I wait for the market to come to me, so I don't have a set trading schedule. I wish I did. But you have to wait for these moves. You can't force it.

You're not in New York City, so tell me how you get your information. Is there a gap between what and when you learn something compared to the market?

My information sources are pretty good. I have a real-time global news source as well as having Bloomberg on all the time. I watch so many things on my charts—they will all tell a story as to what is happening in the world. I don't find that I am at any more of a disadvantage than when I was sitting in an office in Chicago. There are so many people on a trading floor that if something happens, even if you have a squawker, chances are the move has already happened. I guess I am not in the thick of things maybe for "floor gossip." Like "So-and-so is now trading 500 lots" or "So-and-so is making..." I don't care about that stuff, and I am happier away from that kind of atmosphere. I work hard every day to keep myself informed as to what is going on in the markets, but more importantly understanding the markets and staying focused. With today's technology I feel like I am sitting on a trading floor.

Consider a Forex day trader. Does he or she have a real opportunity to make money?

Yes and no. It depends on the person. I do think probably anyone could trade. But the best traders I know aren't the ones with an economics degree, or Ph.D., etc. The best guys are the ones that can smell the blood—a dedication and a love for all markets. If it moves, they will trade it. I wouldn't really advise anyone to just get online and start trading. There are too many factors that power these markets today. They change daily—and you have to change daily. You need to know how to dissect the market every day. That in itself is a full-time job.

8

INSIDE A FOREX
PLATFORM

In the last 10 years, and especially the last five, the Forex market has evolved with amazing speed. Today, the retail trader equipped with just a basic workstation and Internet connection can trade Forex, with the pricing and execution comparable to the interbank market. What historically was the exclusive domain of banks, multinational corporations, and hedge funds is now accessible to investors from Albany to Zurich.

Banks once made sure that Forex information was closely guarded, making the price-discovery process difficult and mistakes to outsiders costly. This inefficient market kept bid/ask spreads wide and transaction costs high. With the rise of computers, however, information can be disseminated among millions of people instantaneously, making execution significantly easier, trades less costly, and the retail trader's market price of a specific currency pair highly accurate.

Despite existing for only a few short years, Forex platforms have become highly sophisticated. They provide investors with a technologically stable, Web-based trading platform, which provides a constant flow of orderly quotes in volatile periods. Figure 8.1 shows a standard, retail trading platform.

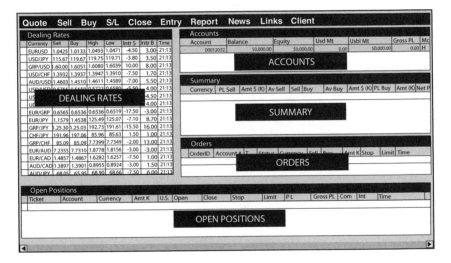

Figure 8.1—A standard, retail trading platform.

The computer code that platforms use today, such as Java, can handle an enormous amount of information without crashing or knocking the user offline. In simple terms, you know that when you log on, the platform will function.

On a single platform, a trader can expect to trade leveraged positions from $10,000 to $25 million without losing execution or price quality. And although there is major room for improvement, most Forex firms today can provide streaming, tradable, two-sided quotes with constant 3-5 pip in spreads.

All these factors make trading Forex today on platforms far less risky than five years ago.

Searching for the Right Platform

A *trading platform* is, in simple terms, the mechanism you use to trade Forex over the Internet. Because of the limited information available, Forex trading platforms share similar features. The most basic transactions are buy, sell, and settle currency pairs (see Figure 8.2). However, not all trading platforms are created equal. Some lack features that I believe are very important. Others have features that suit a specific style of trading (see Figure 8.3).

The first retail Forex platform I ever used to trade retail Forex was called ChoiceFx. It provided only the most basic of trading features—no charts, news, or sophisticated orders like trailing stops and OCO. It did, however, show the depth of the dealer's market, which was great except there was never really any market. Note: A Forex market maker only has access to his/her own "book" and can't see the flow of other market makers such as FCMs or banks. At its core and in its simplicity, this was a very functional platform.

The problem was the dealing desk. Just like platforms today, behind the applications was a person making the prices. I never actually visited Choice FX's dealing room, but I'm sure there weren't more then two dealers for all the currencies (since, every time I called the desk, I would speak with one of two people). They must have eached worked 12-hour shifts. Prices were jumpy at best, spreads were wide, orders were constantly repriced, and—during volatile periods—the dealers would stop quoting altogether. In

Asian trading, you could see where the dealers had fallen asleep as the market price moved away from their price. They would be quoting USD/JPY 132.45 and the market would be 132.75 or higher. I would trade on the price just for the reaction. Inevitably, the phone would ring and the dealer would sheepishly say that they couldn't honor the trade.

Things have changed since then. Today's platforms have the sophistication to fulfill the needs of today's Forex traders and they have the dealing desks to create an orderly and dependable market.

As I've said before, this book doesn't tell you what decision to make in the Forex market. It aims to provide you with the knowledge you need to make the decision that best suits you. Again, any name that appears in this book is by no means an endorsement of that firm.

Figure 8.2 — A typical EBS-style quote window.

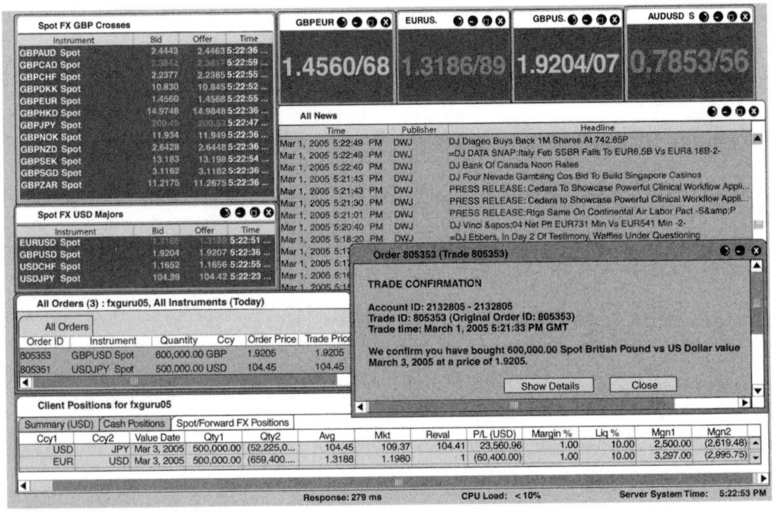

Figure 8.3 — Retail Forex platform with trade confirmation ticket.

Doing Your Homework

As with any important transaction, you want to make sure you're dealing with someone you can trust and rely on. Forex has suffered in the past from scandals and fraud, so it's important to take some elementary steps to protect yourself and your money.

Investors using a Forex firm based in the U.S. should start by checking out the website for the National Futures Association (www.nfa.futures.org). As explained earlier, the NFA is the self-regulatory body given authority by the Commodity Futures Trading Commission.

The NFA's website emphasizes a critical point: "Forex dealers are not all regulated the same way. Only regulated entities such as banks, insurance companies, broker dealer or futures commission merchants, and affiliates of regulated entities may enter into off-exchange Forex trades with retail customers."

This means that all Forex dealers and market makers must be registered with the NFA. However, although the dealers must be regulated, account reps, managers, and other individuals can solicit and manage accounts without being regulated.

I recommend that all investors make sure that they are dealing only with individuals and organizations that have registered. Investors who choose to work with an unregulated firm or individual should be especially careful.

In the NFA's basic broker/firm information section, an investor can research Forex dealers' and brokers' registration status and background and see if there has been any disciplinary action against the firms. Moreover, the NFA website provides breaking-news alerts as well as general background information on the Forex markets.

The Commodity Futures Trading Commission's website www.cftc.gov also provides information on the Forex market, but not to the same extent as the NFA's. It does provide an excellent financial breakdown of all registered Forex and futures FCMs, and it offers a wealth of reassuring data, including net capital. This number gives you an instant understanding of the size of the firms you might be dealing with.

Other excellent websites are www.moneytec.com and www.elite trader.com. These two websites show the international nature of this market and its ability to regulate itself. The chat rooms, where you can communicate with traders halfway around the world, can provide invaluable information. These are informal, self-regulating sites where you can find excellent information on the Forex market. Please, however, take all postings with a grain of salt because not all posters are as altruistic and honest as declared.

Retail Platforms

A Forex platform should be relatively simple and easy to master. When looking at a platform, make sure it's not overly complicated. Although such platforms may appear to offer enormous numbers of features, the reality is that too much design can impede performance—the streaming quotes are jumpy, account updates are slow, and order execution is confusing. When the market starts to move, you don't want to have to figure out what side you're on. Figure 8.4 and 8.5 shows a standard retail trading platforms with an order window.

Figure 8.4—A standard retail trading platform with an order window.

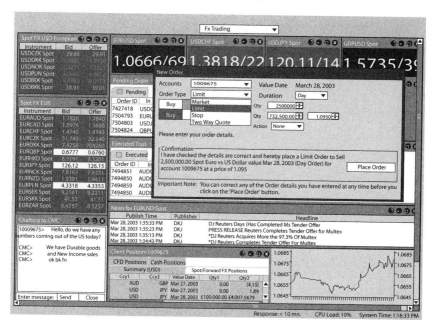

Figure 8.5—Another example of an integrated retail Forex trading platform.

Would you buy a car before taking a test drive? No way. Take advantage of demonstration offers. While doing this, pay considerable attention to your ability to navigate. Don't get caught up in the firm's marketing hype, bells and whistles, bright colors, or "unique" features, because they probably won't make you trade better and could possibly interfere with your strategy.

Sometimes the small things can be the most frustrating. I once traded on a platform where the "open position" window was too small. If I traded too many multiple pairs, I would lose one from the window, making me think a stop had been executed and that my position had closed. On another platform, I confused what side of the market I was on and added to a losing position instead of closing.

I now look for platforms that have a type of "panic" close option. This allows me, no matter what, to enter a close position order and get out. Most non-Forex traders might find this feature strange, but remember that Forex trading often occurs in the early morning after a sleepless (and stressful) night.

The following list describes the items you find on a standard Forex platform:

- **Standard trading windows**

- **Dealing rates**

  Currency pairs—All the available currency pairs that a dealer is prepared to make a market for.

  Sell/buy—A two-sided quote.

  High/low—The highest and lowest price for the trading period.

  Time and date—The time and date that the last quote was posted.

  Interest buy/sell—Some platforms show the interest rate for the pair.

- **Account summary**

  Balance—The total amount of capital.

  Currency—A specific currency pair.

  Used margin—The amount of margin currently in use.

  Usable margin—The amount of margin available.

  Gross P/L—The total amount of profit and loss.

- **Open orders**

  Order type—What type of order was executed, such as market or limit.

  Currency—A specific currency pair.

  Sell/buy—The price at which the order will be executed.

  Amt—The size of the trade.

  Stop—The predetermined stop loss entered.

  Limit—The predetermined limit order.

  Order entry time—The time the order was entered.

- **Open positions**

  Currency—The specific currency pair traded.

  Amount—The position size.

  Sell/buy—What side of the market the trade was made on.

  Open—The price at which the trade was opened.

  Current price—The price at which it closed at market.

  Stop—The price at which a stop order was entered.

  Limit—The price at which a limit order was entered.

  P/L—The profit or loss of the specific trade.

  Commission—The commission charged.

  Interest—The interest gained or lost on the position.

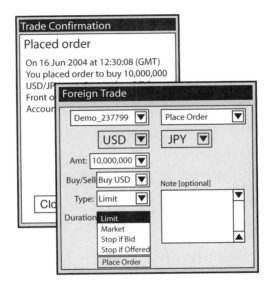

Figure 8.6—An order entry ticket with followup trade confirmation.

The following sections discuss critical features of retail trading platforms.

Trading Mechanisms

Platforms are based on three types of retail trading mechanisms. This is true for both single-market-maker portals, a platform that allows the trader to trade with only one counterparty on one quote, and multicounterparty portals, a platform that allows the trader to choose from multiple quotes and who he trades with. It is important to know the differences between these trading mechanisms because each offers different advantages and drawbacks.

Hub and Spoke Trading

This is used in multicounterparty portals. Each participant in the network posts bids and offers, making a real market. Hub and Spoke trading allows the traders to see other bids and offers from other traders on the platform and allows the trader to choose the counterparty. This provides excellent transparency a market depth and tighter, more competitive pricing, because there is no trading desk and no price manipulation.

The disadvantage of this type of platform is that a liquidity crisis can occur if all the participants decide to trade on one side and there is no one to take the other side of the trade. This can happen if some damaging news hits the market, prompting traders to sell a particular currency. If no one is buying, that currency will drop until a buyer steps in.

Hub and Spoke trading is similar to the process used on the NASDAQ level II with multiple market makers posting bids and offers. Its mechanism gives the trader the closest view of a whole market available today. You will find this trading mechanism in institutional platforms such as Fxall, Currenex, and State Streets Fx Connect.

Three retail platforms offer a version of hub and spoke trading—Hotspotfx (although it is the actual counterparty to all transactions), CoesFX, and GFTs Inter Trader Exchange, which allows traders to trade directly with each other. This trading mechanism is the future of retail Forex trading.

Request for Quote (RFQ)

This process uses an IM (instant message) feature within the trading platform, which connects the traders with the market maker. The trader asks for a quote, generally giving the market maker the currency pair and size of the trade. The market maker replies by quoting a two-sided price. This process favors the market maker over the trader because only the market maker sees the price. The market maker can "lean" on the price—jack it up or down—since only he has time to see the trade and positions before quoting. This is an older trading mechanism; most Forex firms and their clients prefer click and deal. However, for larger trades, $25 million and up, this is the preferred method.

How Common Is Leaning?

When questioned if leaning actually occurs, one dealer agreed to speak off the record on the subject.

"I believe you mean pushing stops. I know at my firm it doesn't happen, and I don't think it's as widespread as the retail traders believe. Slippage and gaps are part of the volatile nature of this market. The CFTC and NFA are taking a very proactive approach toward the retail business, and the market is becoming very transparent. Second, our data feed is being sent to many traders, data providers, and chart providers, and people compare these charts, and if traders see any strange price movement, it can become an issue. Third, at the larger Forex firms there are traders on both sides of the market watching the price action. So, if the price moves too far, they will scalp the market, potentially costing the firm any gain. Perhaps at the smaller Forex firms, a pip or two they might get away with. I can't believe today a firm would stay in business very long if pushing stops occurred on a regular basis."

Click and Deal

Click and deal is also known as "What you click is what you get" (WYC/WYG), one-click dealing, or executable streaming price feed. Click and deal is the most common platform for retail Forex traders. It increases transparency and limits the market makers' advantage. The quotes are live, meaning that they can be instantly traded on. Moreover, most prices are *streamed*, meaning that they are continuously updated and represent a dependable, orderly market. There is a limit to the amount that can be traded on each price, but that limit is more than sufficient for most retail traders.

This platform is transparent because the market maker must post a two-sided quote. The trader has the advantage of seeing a price before showing the dealer his intention, such as trade size and direction. The trader has the benefit of choosing to trade on the posted prices or not. The reverse would be the RFP, where the trader asks the market maker for a price and gives pair and size, and the dealer can adjust the quote accordingly.

Most platforms in the retail Forex world today use the click and deal mechanism. It is a very powerful tool and is perfectly suited for the average retail trader. In addition, by understanding how the system works, you can avoid some of the basic pitfalls and glitches listed later in this chapter.

In this interview, Gary L. Tilkin, a principle at Global Forex Trading—one of the first Forex platforms to use computer technology—talks about the evolution from commodities broker in the mid-1990s, to Forex trades. He begins by describing how the physical handling of orders would often break down under volume pressure.

We had a lot of orders coming in at the same time. It got to the point we were flooding the trading floor with physical paper and guys on the floor were complaining to our clearing floor that it was getting to be this massive flood of order tickets, not event cancel order[s] but also stuff they liked—like market orders. The volume was just getting very tough down there for them to handle. The CME floor was not electronic and not efficient in laying paper very well. So we started to get to the point where it took a long time to get a market order back.

We would have very long delays in replace. Sometimes as long as 20 minutes after you thought you had moved the stop it hadn't yet been moved. It was still at the old price. People were confused; we were confused. Sometimes it would take hours to get the fill back with a stop fill. And that was at the old price and not the new price you thought you had moved at. And we would spend hours after the closing clearing up the confusion. But then we began to lose business. And clients wouldn't get any better service, but in the meantime we would lose them. And I started doing research and found only one other company offering software to do Forex trades. We knew we wanted to be dealers, so we licensed and did it as a deal where we actually held the money.

What year?

1997. This was the year we formed Global Forex Trading [GFT]. And we moved our futures currency business over to this new entity. And what was strange or atypical is everything worked well from day one. Occasionally there was a minor glitch like software would go down for a short period. Considering all the trouble we had on the trading floor, the few glitches we encountered from this solid software was nothing. And clients still were happy. They were delighted in that they could just sit there and click away and trade, never worrying about [how] often they placed cancel replace orders or how long it took. Because it was all almost instantaneous. And it revolutionized our business life almost immediately. And we began to look around for better software and found some, but it lacked the ability to handle the volume we were already doing. We ended up doing a lot of keypunching when it should be automated. So I made the decision— we need to build our own. So at that same time we flew to New York and met with a team of developers. We showed them our ideas, which we had a lot of at that time. And they developed the most sophisticated platform at the time, which is now known as Dealbook Fx, and that was what we called it from the very beginning. We worked the bugs out over the next several months and literally dumped millions into the system and servers. And I don't think even our competitors would dispute that we have the best piece of software on the market today.

Can you talk about some of the features?

Automated trailing stops, the ability to deal off charts, where you can just click the charts and buys and sell can do cancel replace by just dragging the horizontal line that represents the current stop or limit and move it to a new point that effectively cancels the old order almost instantaneously. Click and deal and filled almost instantly. We have advanced charting, where the charting is actually integrated into the dealing interface. It's all one package, so you don't have to run a dealing package and a separated charting package. It has 60 to 70 indicators; some are proprietary. We offer Joe Denapally's indicators that are right from his book and can develop custom indicators of individuals and now have the ability for clients to design their own indicators and also enter orders off those generated signals. Of course, it has alarms that send signals to cell phones or PDA or e-mail. You can set them on indicators and/or prices.

It is completely head and shoulders above the original technology we introduced in 1997. One thing we decided at GFT was that our technology would differentiate us from our competitors. We will listen to customers, we will watch what the market is offering, and we will look internally for new features.

The third part is the dealing, which is incredible and allows dealers to operate very efficiently. We can have multiple data feeds flowing through it. We can execute orders with counterparties of our own, such as banks in the interbank.

The following sections discuss other important platform features.

News

News feeds tend to be a misleading feature, because most web-based news lags the market. Indicators tend to be broadcast after the information has already spread among investors. In a market where seconds can mean the difference between a profit and a loss, this is a major disadvantage for some traders. If your trading style is based on fundamentals or is event-driven, you should invest in a high-level feed that will keep up with the markets. However, if your strategy is to just use the news as an indicator, utilize the free news feed provided by your broker and combine it with a TV business news channel such as Bloomberg.

Charts

A good charting package is essential for successful trading and is a standard feature with most Forex accounts. Like any investment chart, it visually represents historical price data. In addition, it lets investors manipulate data by timescale and period, by currency pairs, and by technical indicators. Because of the lack of information in Forex (such as market depth and trade size), charts become your eyes and ears on the currency market.

An important factor to consider about Forex charts is their data feed. In other words, where does the price data come from? A variety of sources can give you information, but since there is no one centralized Forex market, no one is necessarily better than another. Reuters and EBS, because they are used in interbank pricing, might better represent the true market. But these are very expensive. Most retail traders can use a single charting platform with backup reference charts to refer to.

Remember, without a centralized market, no two price feeds and their charts are exactly alike. Since charts are the trader's lifeline to the market, you should seriously consider purchasing another "stand-alone" charting package such as tradestation. Compare the two, and make sure you are getting fast and accurate data.

Research

Most platforms today provide some kind of research. This is a mixed blessing. On the one hand, it provides additional market insight and alternative points of view, but on the other hand, it's easy to rely too much on that information when making a trade.

To avoid this trap, traders should review information from several independent sources and always keep an open mind. As a general rule, I avoid analyst reports from an FCM—or I at least read them with a healthy dose of skepticism. As with any source, ask questions. From whom and where is this information? Forex does not have the regulator oversight that is common in other markets, so there can be an enormous disparity about what is said and reported. Remember, the objective of an FCM analyst is to generate trading— not necessarily returns.

If you are looking for reliable reports on the Forex markets, stick to the major banks. Be careful on the Web. Some sites are reliable, but others should be read skeptically. Websites such as www.fxstreet.com (an amazing Forex resource that I highly recommend) offer a free and varied list of information providers.

Figure 8.7 shows an integrated retail trading platform that includes prices, orders, news, and charts.

Spot TxBR Comp			Spot Market			EURO/USD Spot	CHF/USD Spot
Instrument	Bid	Offer	Instrument	Bid	Offer		
EURAUD Spot	1.7839	1.7859	EUR/USD Spot	1.0507	1.0570	1.0567/70	1.5677/8
EURCAD Spot	1.7839	1.7859	GEP/USD Spot	1.5886	1.5676		
EURCHF Spot	1.7839	1.7859	USD/CHF Spot	1.2786	1.2785		
EURCCK Spot	1.7839	1.7859	USD/JPY Spot	1.1507	1.0571		
EURDKKSpot	1.7839	1.7859	Spot EURO/Market			USD/CHF Spot	USD/JPY Spot
EURGEP Spot	1.7839	1.7859	Instrument	Bid	Offer		
EURRKD Spot	1.7839	1.7859	EURUSD Spot	1.0507	1.0570	1.3963/67	121.00/0
EURJPY Spot	1.7839	1.7859	GEPUSD Spot	1.5886	1.5676		
EURROK Spot	1.7839	1.7859	USDCHF Spot	1.2786	1.2785		
EURPUN Spot	1.7839	1.7859	USDJPY Spot	1.1507	1.0571		
EURSBK Spot	1.7839	1.7859					

Executed Transfers (1)

☐ Executed ☐ Pending ☐ Contingent

Order ID	Instrument	Quantity	Ccy	Trade Price	Order Time	Account ID	Buy/Sell	Order Type
7437428	USD/JPY Spot	250.00	USD	120.60	Mar 21 2003 10 29 3	10009675	Sell	Market
7422773	AUDOSP Spot	100.00	AUO	0.3395	Mar 21 2003 6 11 25	10009675	Buy	Market
7422185	AUD/USD Back Ou	150.00	AUO	0.5925570	Mar 21 2003 2 22 58	10009675	Buy	Rollover

Cash Positions Spot,Forward Fx Positions

Summary (USD)				CPD Positions		Spot British Pound vs US Dollar 1 Minute Bid Price Chart
Ccy	Amount	Level	USD Equiv	Type	Notes	
AUD	345.00	0.5919	294.26	Cash		1.5680
GBP	(4.719.62)	1.5681	(7,400.85)	Cash		1.5655
HKD	(100.00)	7.7994	(12.82)	Cash		1.5630

Chatting to CS

| IX7007: | Can I ask you a question? |
| CS: | Hi, this is CS how can I help you? |

Enter message: [   ] [Send] [Close]

News for GRPUSD Spot

Publish Time	Publisher	Headline
Mar 21, 2000 1 49:07 PM	DMJ	DJ Hot Stocks To Watch
Mar 21, 2000 1 45:53 PM	DMJ	DJ Co-loa Command Bristling -2 New
Mar 21, 2000 1 44:43 PM	DMJ	DJ Ashbead Group Pays Deferred Interest Pay
Mar 21, 2000 1 43:33 PM	DMJ	DJ CORRECT WS-UK Forces Advance in South
Mar 21, 2000 1 39:23 PM	DMJ	DJ Carnival Corp Earnings To Hold Conf

Figure 8.7—An integrated retail trading platform with prices, orders, news, and charts.

Things to Look Out For

Of course, no platform is perfect.

Requotes

Requotes occur when you accept a price and the dealer pulls away the original quote. It can happen with any mechanism, but it should be a concern if it occurs too often. Requotes typically occur in a fast-moving market when your decision to trade on the given quote was too slow. It also can happen because your dealer is underhanded. He sees your trade, and it's easy for him to make some free pips by altering the quote in his favor.

Technology has advanced to the point that requotes should be very rare in a stable market. Any more than a few requotes should be considered sketchy and be immediately addressed. Unfortunately, if you feel that you lost a price because of a requote, there is not much you can do. I have never heard of a trader winning an argument with a broker. The best solution is to keep your eye on alternate price streams, and if requotes occur too often, get a new platform.

Network Connection

Currently, all platforms are Web based, which lends itself to connection problems, meaning the ability for your trading platform to stay connected with your Forex firm. Disconnections can range in time and frequency. Infrequent short-term connection problems are still common, but anything more should be addressed. Traders should look for an easy-to-read indicator showing if the data stream on the platform is connected or not.

Getting the Best Price

How do you search for prices in a decentralized market? How do you know you've found the best one? Forex is made up of hundreds of smaller markets. Thanks to technology, however, these markets are getting linked, so finding the best price is becoming easier. EBS and Reuters have done much to create a centralized market, and most quotes are derived from them. They are also mostly fair, since the law of efficient markets quickly punishes any price that's out of line.

Before this system was developed, voice brokers would search the globe, looking for victims with inadequate information. Although most large Forex participants are protected from any real damage, the retail trader is not, because he can trade with only a single counterparty. The trader is at the mercy of the market maker to provide competitive prices and tight spreads. If he doesn't, the trader has no other recourse than to close the account and find a better provider.

Straight-through processing (STP) is the ideal process for the retail trading platform. STP means that there is zero interaction between the time the trade is placed and the time it is accepted. There is no room for trade manipulation or order mistakes.

Spreads can widen and prices become volatile after:

- A Central Bank rate or monetary decision

- An unpredicted event creates market instability and volatility

- Volatile market conditions

- Illiquid market conditions

Safety

This should be a major concern for anyone trading over an open network such as the Internet. High-speed Internet connections give you enormous access to information, but they can also make you more vulnerable to viruses, worms, and hackers.

Take these problems seriously. Buy the proper software to protect yourself, and keep it updated. Make sure you set your PC's firewall to an appropriate setting.

My Trading Room

After you've selected a retail platform, consider setting up a place in your home to trade from. A quiet spot in the house where you can shut the door is optimal. You will require an Internet connection that is fast and reliable. This will be your connection to the market and the world, and you don't want a weak rope. It will also be helpful to have a television set with access to 24-hour news channels as well as business channels.

Although you should not trade on the news you get from TV, because even a few minutes of delay will leave you behind the market, the news will help clarify any major event and give you a better understanding of price changes in the market. Most Forex platforms provide charting software and a news stream as a courtesy, but it is in an investor's best interest to find an independent source of quotes. This is because the prices reflect only the single FCM's or market maker's view of the market, which at times might not be in synch with other market makers. Having multiple price streams gives you a better idea of what you are trading against.

Information Sources

Information is crucial to any investor in any market, but it's especially true of the Forex market, where billions of dollars can be won or lost in a day on a single news item. Many retail trade platforms are good information sources, providing real-time news, in-depth features, and advice on how to invest.

Several financial websites are also excellent sources of news in real time. They include Bloomberg (www.bloomberg.com; registration is required for access to some portions of the site), CBS MarketWatch (www.marketwatch.com; it is free, but registration is required), and Reuters (www.reuters.com; it is free). Another website, Thomson (www.thomson.com), is for more sophisticated investors and provides real-time news and investing advice for a fee.

Any investor must be ready to do a minimum of reading every day to keep up with the Forex markets. Because of the international flavor of the Forex markets, simply reading the *Wall Street Journal*, the *New York Times*, and *Business Week* magazine won't be enough.

Check out news sources based in Great Britain. This includes the daily newspaper the *Financial Times,* an excellent source of international reporting and commentary, the BBC (www.bbc.com), and the magazine the *Economist.* Note that all of these organizations can be accessed for free or by subscription over the Internet.

Many traders keep the TV on while investing, because access to real-time news is essential. If it's available, check out the Bloomberg channel. Another more mainstream business channel is CNBC.

For more focused information on the Forex markets, a number of free sites exist. Take a look at www.forexstreet.com, www.forexnews.com, and www.globalview.com, which is a chat room where traders around the world swap information. But beware that many Forex sites are affiliated with trading firms. Although I don't believe they distort information, they might not give you the full story.

As you become more experienced, you will learn how to get information from several different sources. The important thing is not to get into a rut. Mix it up, change the channel, check out a different magazine, subscribe to a different newspaper, surf a different website. After all, the market is always changing, and the best way to anticipate change is to prevent yourself from getting too comfortable and believing you know more than you truly do.

Important Numbers

You should have on hand a list of phone numbers of customer representatives, brokers, back-office staff, and the dealing desk. Make sure that in the event of a power outage or a discrepancy in a trade, you can *immediately* dial a number and get a person at the other end, 24 hours a day. Don't say something like "Well, I can always go to their website and get contacts there." You need to have these numbers literally at your fingertips. If something occurs during a trade—such as price spikes—and you are knocked off the platform, you need to call immediately. Or, during a power outage, when you have live trades on the market, the only thing that will keep your trading strategy intact will be your backup communication system.

Forex Retail Platforms

Before I describe specific Forex trading platforms and corresponding Forex firms, I need to stress that this book doesn't endorse any particular platform. Nor do I make judgments regarding the quality of service or prices. I provide current information, but you're responsible for doing the final research and making your own decision based on that information.

In the last five years, the quality and selection of retail platforms have increased significantly. While as of 2004 no major financial institution directly offered a Forex platform, some banks have strategic partnerships with existing Forex firms. Large trading firms historically known for futures trading—such as Man Financial and Refco—have moved into the market, providing a new level of investor security.

Moreover, online trading firms that were developed for daytrading equities in the '90s have aggressively begun to move into the Forex market. This recent push into the Forex market, along with older firms developing sophisticated trading technology after years of client interaction, gives the Forex investor a wealth of choices.

You should pay particular attention to the counterparty to your transaction. This is a major consideration in the interbank market and should be considered a risk on the retail level. The firms listed here are registered FCMs and, therefore, make their own markets. Other firms, such as Tradestation, concentrate on developing stable, fast Forex trading software and use another firm as the counterparty.

Forex Trading Platforms

The following lists Forex trading platforms (and this list is growing daily).

Company name: SNC Investments, Inc.
Website: www.sncinvestment.com
Year the company was founded: 2003
Commissions: None
Minimum investment: $500
Minimum transaction: $10,000
Pip spread: 4 to 5 pips
Tradeable pairs: Majors
Customers: Individual investors, institutions
Languages: English, French, Japanese, Korean
Free demo account: Yes
Mini Forex trading: Yes
24-hour trading: Yes
Regulated by: National Futures Association/Commodity Futures Trading Commission
Headquarters: 101 California St. #3050, San Francisco, CA 94111

Company name: FX Solutions LLC
Website: www.fxsol.com
Year the company was founded: 2000
Commissions: No commission on Forex
Minimum investment: $300 for a mini account
Minimum transaction: $1,000
Pip spread: 3 to 5 pips
Tradeable pairs: EUR/USD, USD/JPY, GBP/USD, USD/CHF, USD/CAD, AUD/USD, EUR/GBP, EUR/JPY, EUR/CHF, GBP/JPY
Customers: Corporate, financial institutions, fund managers, CTAs, CPOs, introducing brokers, private investors

Languages: English, Spanish, Chinese
Free demo account: Yes
Mini Forex trading: Yes
24-hour trading: Yes
Regulated by: National Futures Association/Commodity Futures Trading Commission
Headquarters: 127 East Ridgewood, Suite 201, Ridgewood, NJ 07450

Company name: Socofinance SA
Website: www.socofinance.com
Year the company was founded: 1978
Commissions: No commission on Forex
Minimum investment: $10,000
Minimum transaction: $50,000
Pip spread: 2 to 5 pips
Tradeable pairs: Majors
Customers: Banks, private investors
Languages: English, Spanish, German, French, Italian, Arabic, Russian
Free demo account: Yes
Mini Forex trading: No
24-hour trading: Yes
Regulated by: Association Romande des Intermediares Financiers (ARIF)
Headquarters: 20, Rte De Pres Bois, 1215 Geneva 15, Switzerland

Company name: Capital Market Services LLC
Website: www.cmsfx.com
Year the company was founded: 1999
Commissions: No commission on Forex
Minimum investment: $200
Minimum transaction: $10,000
Pip spread: 3 to 4 pips

Tradeable pairs: EUR/USD, USD/JPY, GBP/USD, USD/CHF, EUR/CHF, AUD/USD, USD/CAD, EUR/GBP, EUR/JPY, GBP/JPY, EUR/CAD, EUR/AUD, GBP/CHF, CHF/JPY, AUD/CAD, AUD/JPY, NZD/USD, CAD/JPY

Languages: English, Spanish, German, French, Italian, Portuguese, Chinese, Japanese, Korean, Arabic, Russian, Polish, Taiwanese, Mandarin, Cantonese

Free demo account: Yes

Mini Forex trading: Yes

24-hour trading: Yes

Regulated by: National Futures Association/Commodity Futures Trading Commission

Headquarters: Empire State Building, 350 Fifth Ave., 64th Floor, Suite 6400, New York, NY 10118

Company name: ACM Advanced Currency Markets SA

Website: www.ac-markets.com

Year the company was founded: 2002

Commissions: No commission on Forex

Minimum investment: $5,000

Minimum transaction: $100,000

Pip spread: 3 pips on all majors

Tradeable pairs: EUR/USD, USD/JPY, USD/CHF, GBP/USD, EUR/JPY, EUR/CHF, EUR/GBP, AUD/USD, USD/CAD, AUD/JPY, USD/NOK, USD/SEK

Customers: Private investors, introducing brokers, fund managers, financial institutions, banks

Languages: English, Spanish, German, French, Italian, Portuguese, Arabic, Russian, Greek

Free demo account: Yes

Mini Forex trading: No

24-hour trading: Yes
Regulated by: Swiss Federal Department of Finance
Headquarters: Geneva, Switzerland
Company name: MG Financial Group
Website: www.mgforex.com
Year the company was founded: 1992
Commissions: Commission-free trading
Minimum investment: $1,000
Minimum transaction: $10,000
Pip spread: 3 to 5 pips
Tradeable pairs: Majors
Customers: Individuals, money managers, referring brokers, corporations
Languages: English, Spanish, French, Chinese, Russian, Urdu
Free demo account: Yes
Mini Forex trading: Yes
24-hour trading: Yes
Regulated by: National Futures Association/Commodity Futures Trading Commission
Headquarters: 40 Exchange Place, 12th Floor, New York, NY 10005
Company name: CMC FOREX—CMC GROUP
Website: www.CMCforex.com
Year the company was founded: 1989
Commissions: 100 percent commission-free; 100 to 1 leverage
Minimum investment: $500
Minimum transaction: $10,000 (flexible)
Pip spread: 3 to 4 pips on world majors
Tradeable pairs: 62 pairs available
Customers: Novice, intermediate, experienced individual/corporate traders. IB program: CTAs, brokerage firms, and other financial institutions.

Languages: English, Spanish, Chinese, Russian

Free demo account: Yes

Mini Forex trading: Yes

24-hour trading: Yes

Regulated by: Member of NFA (USA), authorized and regulated by FSA (UK), regulated by ASIC (AUS)

Headquarters: 66 Prescot St., London E1 8HG

Company name: Saxo Bank A/S

Website: www.saxobank.com

Year the company was founded: 1992

Commissions: No commission on Forex

Minimum investment: $10,000

Minimum transaction: $50,000

Pip spread: 2 to 3 pips

Tradeable pairs: Over 120 tradeable pairs, including G7 and exotics

Customers: Corporate, financial institutions, fund managers, introducing brokers, private investors

Languages: English, Spanish, German, French, Italian, Portuguese, Dutch/Flemish, Chinese, Japanese, Korean, Arabic, Russian, Hebrew, Danish, Polish, Greek

Free demo account: Yes

Mini Forex trading: No

24-hour trading: Yes

Regulated by: The Financial Services Authority (FSA), Denmark

Headquarters: Smakkedalen 2, 2820 Gentofte, Denmark

Company name: GCI Financial, Ltd.

Website: www.gcitrading.com

Year the company was founded: 1996

Commissions: No commission on Forex

Minimum investment: $2,000; $500 mini account

Minimum transaction: $10,000

Pip spread: 3 to 5 pips

Tradeable pairs: EUR/USD, USD/JPY, USD/CHF, GPB/USD, EUR/YEN, EUR/JPY, EUR/GBP, EUR/CHF, GBP/JPY, GBP/CHF, CHF/JPY, AUD/USD, AUD/JPY, USD/CAD, NZD/USD, USD/ZAR, USD/NOK, EUR/AUD, GBP/AUD

Customers: Corporations, money managers, institutional investors, individual investors

Languages: English, Spanish, German, French, Chinese, Arabic, Russian

Free demo account: Yes

Mini Forex trading: Yes

24-hour trading: Yes

Regulated by: International Financial Services Commission, British Virgin Islands

Headquarters: DataPro Park, 13.5 Mile North Highway, Ladyville, Belize

Company name: Global Forex Trading

Website: www.gftforex.com

Year the company was founded: 1997

Commissions: No commission on Forex

Minimum investment: $2,500

Minimum transaction: $100,000

Pip spread: 3 to 5 pips

Tradeable pairs: USD/JPY, USD/CHF, GBP/USD, EUR/USD, GBP/JPY, AUD/USD, USD/CAD, USD/NOK, USD/NZD, USD/SEK, USD/ZAR, AUD/CAD, AUD/JPY, CHF/JPY, EUR/AUD, EUR/CAD, EUR/CHF, EUR/GBP, EUR/JPY, GBP/CHF, USD/THB, NZD/JPY, EUR/PLN, EUR/HUF, AUD/CHF, AUD/NZD, AUD/SGD, CAD/CHF, CAD/JPY, CHF/NOK, CHF/SEK, GBP/CAD, GBP/DKK, GBP/HUF, GBP/NOK, GBP/NZD, GBP/PLN, GBP/SEK, GBP/SGD,

GBP/AUD, NOK/SEK, NZD/CAD, NZD/CHF, NZD/DKK, NDZ/SEK, NZD/SGD, USD/CZK, USD/DKK, USD/HUF, USD/MXN, USD/PLN, USD/SGD, EUR/SEK, USD/KRW, EUR/KRW, JPY/KRW, SGD/JPY, THB/JPY, EUR/ZAR, EUR/NOK

Customers: Private investors, introducing brokers, corporate and financial institutions, fund managers

Languages: English, Spanish, Chinese, Japanese, Polish

Free demo account: Yes

Mini Forex trading: No

24-hour trading: Yes

Regulated by: NFA, CFTC (U.S.), ASIC (Australia)

Headquarters: 4760 Fulton Road, Suite 201, Ada, MI 49301

Company name: Forex Capital Markets LLC (FXCM)

Website: www.fxcm.com

Year the company was founded: 1999

Commissions: No commission on Forex

Minimum investment: $2,000

Minimum transaction: $100,000

Pip spread: 3 to 5 pips

Tradeable Pairs: EUR/USD, EUR/CHF, USD/JPY, EUR/CAD, USD/CHF, EUR/AUD, USD/CAD, GBP/JPY, GBP/USD, GBP/CHF, EUR/JPY, CHF/JPY, AUD/USD, AUD/CAD, NZD/USD, AUD/JPY, EUR/GBP, AUD/NZD, NZD/JPY

Customers: FXCM Group has more than 20,000 clients

Languages: English, Spanish, German, French, Italian, Portuguese, Dutch/Flemish, Chinese, Japanese, Korean, Arabic, Russian, Tagalog, Hebrew, Farsi, Afrikaans

Free demo account: Yes

Mini Forex trading: Yes

24-hour trading: Yes

Regulated by: National Futures Association/Commodity Futures Trading Commission

Headquarters: Financial Square, 32 Old Slip, New York, NY 10005

Company name: FOREX.com (an affiliate of GAIN Capital Group)

Website: www.forex.com

Year the company was founded: 1999 (part of GAIN Capital Group)

Commissions: No commission on Forex

Minimum investment: $250 mini, $2,500 standard

Minimum transaction: $10,000

Pip spread: 3 to 5 pips

Tradeable pairs: EUR/USD, USD/JPY, GBP/USD, USD/CHF, USD/CAD, AUD/USD, EUR/JPY, EUR/GBP, EUR/CHF, GBP/JPY, AUD/JPY, CHF/JPY, EUR/AUD, GBP/CHF

Customers: Individuals, money managers, brokerage firms

Languages: English, Chinese, Russian

Free demo account: Yes

Mini Forex trading: Yes

24-hour trading: Yes

Regulated by: National Futures Association/Commodity Futures Trading Commission

Headquarters: U.S.

Company name: Man Financial Limited

Website: www.tradeatman.co.uk

Year the company was founded: The Man Group can trace its origins to 1783, when James Man established a sugar-brokering business in London. Man Group PLC is now an FTSE 100 company (EMG.L), and Man Financial is the world's largest independent futures broker.

Commissions: Spot FX is commission-free

Minimum investment: $20,000

Minimum transaction: Spot $250,000

Pip spread: 3 to 5 pips

Tradeable pairs: EUR/GBP, EUR/JPY, EUR/USD, EUR/CHF, GBP/USD, GBP/JPY, USD/JPY, USD/CHF, USD/CAD, USD/SGP, AUD/USD, AUD/JPY, AUD/NZD, NZD/USD, NZD/JPY

Languages: English, Italian

Free demo account: Yes

Mini Forex trading: No

24-hour trading: Yes

Regulated by: The Financial Services Authority (FSA), United Kingdom

Headquarters: Sugar Quay, Lower Thames St., London EC3R 6DU

Company name: Refco FX

Website: www.refcofx.com

Year the company was founded: 1982

Commissions: No commission on Forex

Minimum investment: $300

Minimum transaction: $10,000

Pip spread: 3 to 5 pips

Tradeable pairs: EUR/USD, USD/JPY, USD/CHF, USD/CAD, GBP/USD, EUR/JPY, AUD/USD, NZD/USD, EUR/GBP, EUR/CHF, EUR/CAD, EUR/AUD, GBP/JPY, GBP/CHF, CHF/JPY, AUD/CAD, AUD/JPY, AUD/NZD, NZD/JPY, CAD/JPY

Customers: The Refco Group has more than 180,000 clients.

Languages: English, Spanish, German, French, Italian, Portuguese, Dutch/Flemish, Chinese, Japanese, Korean, Arabic, Russian, Tagalog, Hebrew, Farsi, Afrikaans

Free demo account: Yes
Mini Forex trading: Yes
24-hour trading: Yes
Regulated by: National Futures Association/Commodity Futures Trading Commission
Headquarters: Financial Square, 32 Old Slip, New York, NY 10005
Company name: HotSpot FX
Website: www.Hotspotfx.com
Year the company was founded: 2000
Commissions: $3 per 100,000 base currency units
Minimum investment: $7,500
Minimum transaction: $100,000
Tradeable Pairs: EUR/USD, GBP/USD, USD/JPY, USD/CHF, USD/CAD, AUD/USD, EUR/JPY, EUR/GBP, EUR/CHF, USD/PLN, EUR/PLN
Free demo account: Yes
Mini Forex trading: Yes
24-hour trading: Yes
Regulated by: National Futures Association/Commodity Futures Trading Commission
Headquarters: 1375 Plainfield Ave., Watchung, NJ 07069

Protecting Yourself

Since the introduction of the Commodity Futures Modernization Act (CFMA) in 2000, the CFTC has the jurisdiction and authority to investigate firms offering or selling foreign exchange futures, options, and even spot products. The CFTC has made great strides in cleaning up this market. It has issued advisory warnings—especially concerning sales solicitations that appear in newspapers, radio, television promotions, or on websites and that promise high-return, low-risk investment opportunities in Forex. Even though Forex is a new market to most investors, that is not an excuse to suspend common sense. In this book, or anywhere else, there are no golden trading secrets. Even if there were, people would not reveal such secrets for $100 per month. The CFTC and NFA urge the public to be skeptical of such claims. They offer some signs to look for and preventive measures that investors can take as they enter the Forex market.

Avoiding Fraud

Generally speaking, foreign currency futures and options contracts may be traded legally on an exchange or board of trade that has been approved by the CFTC. Even where currency trading does not occur on a commission-approved exchange or board of trade, it can be conducted legally. In such a case, generally speaking, one or both parties to the trade must be (or must be a regulated affiliate of) a bank, insurance company, registered securities broker-dealer, futures commission merchant or other financial institution, or an individual or entity with a high net worth.

Where Forex firms do not fall into these categories of regulated entities and engage in foreign currency futures and options transactions with or for retail customers who do not have a high net worth, the CFTC has jurisdiction over those firms and their transactions.

If you are solicited by a company that claims to trade foreign currencies and asks you to commit funds for those purposes, you should be very careful. Watch for the warning signs listed in the following sections, and take the recommended precautions before placing your funds with any currency trading company.

The Firm Promises a Free Lunch

Remember, there's no such thing. If a scheme promises quick riches with little effort, then be aware because it might be a fraud. Investing has always attracted a criminal element that can ensnare the unsuspecting or the naïve. This is especially true of inexperienced people who have just received a windfall—from a retirement or the sale of a home—and are eager to invest it somewhere. Some telltale signs are firms that "guarantee" profits or a high return. They'll use lines like, "Whether the market moves up or down, in the currency market you will make a profit," or, "The main advantage of the Forex markets is that there is no bear market." Remember, the investment pros on Wall Street are thrilled to beat the markets by one or two percentage points—and even that achievement is relatively rare and even they suffer down years. Anyone who does not acknowledge this reality should not be handling your money and you should never believe any firm that says, "With a $10,000 deposit, the maximum you can lose is $200 to $250 per day."

The Trader Uses Terminology You Don't Fully Understand

Do you remember the commercials that used to appear on television? "It's five o'clock. Do you know what your child is doing?" An investor should be thinking, "Do I know what my money is doing?" If you don't, then you are far more likely to lose it. This does not mean that you are necessarily being cheated. Many legitimate investing strategies can put you at greater risk, but you must be aware of it and be ready to accept the chance of greater losses. A perfect example is margin trading. Currency traders may ask for money from investors to trade on "margin." As we explain elsewhere in this book, margin allows a mere $1,000 to $5,000 to control vastly larger sums on the Forex markets. It increases the size of the reward but also increases the size of the pain if the market goes against you. Consequently, an investor may give a relatively small amount to a trader and find himself or herself facing far greater losses. This goes for any other trading strategy or vocabulary. If your trader is using terminology that you don't fully grasp, then you should not be risking your money.

The Firm Claims To Trade in the "Interbank Market"

Some firms or companies will say that they have access to the "interbank market" and can therefore trade at better prices on your behalf. This is a sign of possible fraud and you should remember our first warning sign—someone is offering you a free lunch. The interbank market is dominated by large institutions—banks, corporations, and financial powerhouses. Anyone who claims to have that kind of access should be closely questioned.

The Firm is Using the Hard Sell via the Internet

The Internet, as we have noted, has greatly increased the individual's ability to access financial information and trade relatively quickly and at low prices. The downside of this is that it has also made it easier (and cheaper) to use fraudulent and misleading pitches to reach investors and take their money from them. Be careful of a hard sell that is followed with pressure to transfer funds quickly over the Internet. In many cases, sending money can be as easy as clicking a button, but getting it back can be almost impossible. Be especially aware of firms that do not conspicuously list their addresses. If they are not located in the U.S., then your money could be sent to a foreign firm, and it may be virtually impossible to recover.

The Firm is Vague and Little Information is Available

The good news is that a certain measure of due diligence can protect you from most scams. If you are considering sending your money to a firm, get as much information about the firm as possible—especially about their track record with other clients. If the firm is vague or is unwilling to send you this information, this should be your first warning sign. However, even if they do send you a packet of information that appears professional, be careful that it is not fraudulent.

Another way to ensure that a firm is legitimate is to do background checks on the people running it. A simple Internet search can yield enormous amounts of information. Use this to confirm that the firm's statements are true. Do not rely on what the company tells or promises you. Above all, if you feel any suspicion about the firm, trust it. There are plenty of legitimate Forex firms that will give you the trading opportunities you seek.

9

TRADING INSIDE THE 24-HOUR STORM

The Forex market is often considered a traders' marketplace. This refers to the belief that mastering the skills of disciplined trading is better than trying to specifically understand Forex's chaotic behavior. The theory is that if you are already good at trading in another investment market, with a few minor adjustments, Forex will come naturally as well.

Working Around the Clock

Forex is a 24-hours-a-day market. I cannot stress this enough. It transforms the trading dynamic into an emotional exercise and a physical challenge. It is true that other markets have developed 24-hour capabilities, but none has the sophistication and reach of Forex.

You are trading the stock of a nation, so in any country, such as Japan, Australia, or Turkey, desks of traders are ready to trade during their "normal" trading hours. Only a few hours out of any 24-hour period can be described as light, and even then there is sufficient liquidity to handle any retail order (see Figure 9.1). This gives dedicated retail Forex traders an attractive investment market to trade in, with increased opportunities.

You should carefully manage physical stress. Stress is your enemy in any trading environment, but it can become amplified through the long Forex hours. If you don't manage your physical and emotional levels effectively, your trading performance can be negatively affected, and it may even become dangerous to your health. Round-the-clock trading takes a toll on your body and mind. It's hard to see clearly unless you can control your stress. Take the time to understand how these factors affect you. You must know later, with a lot of money on the line, that you have the skill and endurance to meet the demands of the Forex market.

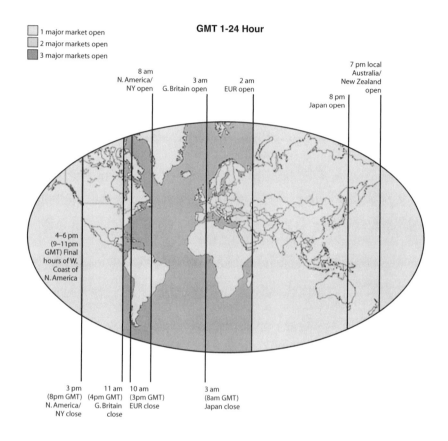

Figure 9.1—Not restricted by exchanges, Forex is truly global. The USD trading in Hong Kong is the exact same USD trading in New York. This lack of an open and close must be examined by all Forex traders.

Defining Your Trading Strategy

Every trade should be part of a thought-out strategy. A strategy gives you the discipline to ride winners and cut losers and even adjust to an unforeseen event. Only expert, seasoned trading veterans should trade on a "feeling." At that point most would tell

you they have identified a unique strategy that works. Otherwise, "feelings" are often just personal biases that cloud the decision-making process.

The best traders always write out their trading strategy before they enter any market. This prevents them from searching for trades or rationalizing a trade by analyzing previously unrelated data. Objective analyses must be done before the trade is entered into the market. Once the trade is placed, the trader has a vested interest in the outcome, and this affects the decision-making process. In the worst case, this vested interest blinds the trader when the environment turns against him.

Every trading strategy should have the following basic elements:

- **Entry point**—The price at which the strategy gets initiated.

- **Exit point**—The expectation of returns on a trade.

- **Stop loss**—The expected downside loss.

- **Limit order (riding stop)**—A movable order that lets you capture returns in a fast-moving market.

This combination of elements is a template that can be used for any and every trade.

Contingency Plans

Rapid change in the Forex market must be factored into trading strategies. A market that spans the globe is also vulnerable to an increased number of unexpected events that can suddenly and decisively change the trading landscape. It could be a terrorist bomb, the death of a government official, or a surprise international merger. These events can prompt you to enter the market aggressively, hold back on a trade, or redefine your strategy

(which I generally discourage, although there are times when it is appropriate). When contemplating any trade, review possible positive and negative events and the corresponding actions should they occur.

Cut Losers

This simple concept is probably the most difficult to put into practice. Undisciplined traders quickly discard their predetermined exit point in the hopes of a quick reversal, allowing a bad trade to snowball. Moreover, every trader has seen his stops hit multiple times, only to see the market then move in his direction. After seeing this a few times, even disciplined traders often diverge from their strategy and remove the stops.

In these cases, traders have rejected an effective tool in Forex: the stop loss. Stops are placed to control downside risk. They are trip wires that save your position if the market moves against you. Not all trades are profitable. The key is strictly managing your money so that if you have a wrong trade you can trade again.

Pigs Get Slaughtered

This is an adage on Wall Street, but I think it applies equally to Forex. The Forex market can often fluctuate with large moves, and when you are on the right side of that move, there is nothing worse than getting out too early. On the other hand, however, holding a trade too long, until your profit has dwindled to nothing, or perhaps a negative trade at a loss, can damage your psyche. It's all right to leave money on the table when you have made your expected returns. The key is following your broader money strategy—to define exactly how much return you are expecting on every trade and, in the case where the market is moving in your favor, installing trailing stops to protect gains that will save your money.

Overleveraging and Overtrading

The lure of high leverage in the Forex market is powerful, but traders should be very careful with their money management. Just because you can find a firm that will give you 400 to 1 does not mean you should use it. As I've said before, leverage is a double-edged sword: Although the gains can be substantial, so can the losses. Just because a trader can leverage $1,000 into a $100,000 lot doesn't mean a trader with $10,000 should invest all he has in 10 lots. The biggest problem with overleveraging is that traders are forced to exit a position prematurely.

Another common mistake is overtrading an account. A basic rule is no more than 5 percent of account value per trade. Depending on risk tolerance and time horizon, this number can be adjusted slightly. Longer-term trades should be a lower percentage, and short-term trades should be higher.

Watch the Markets

The Forex market is the most interconnected market in the world. Each currency is affected by the movement of every other currency. This triggers a web of reactions and counterreactions. When there is social unrest in Sudan, the currency markets move on the news first. In the 1980s, South Africa's devastating policy of apartheid affected the nation's currency, the rand, which fluctuated violently whenever someone was killed in a public political protest.

These factors cause a wealth of opportunities as well as enormous downside risk. For a well-versed trader, a scan of the world's currency markets can uncover incredible possibilities, but for the narrow-minded trader, this is too broad a scope.

Don't Walk Away

I often hear technical traders say, "Put a trade in and walk away." I think this is the equivalent of trading suicide. In the currency markets, wild fluctuations are normal. Spikes occur daily, caused by a fundamental event or large trades hitting the market. Whenever you put a trade in the marketplace, I advise that you actively monitor it.

Remember, you can lose more than your initial investments in the Forex market. Because a currency cannot go down to zero, you have an incentive to watch all your trades. An extreme example is from 1997, when a few Asian governments devalued their currency with no official advance notice. If you were on the wrong side of that trade, you were responsible for all the losses. Some Forex firms advertise guaranteed spots, giving the retail investor a false sense of security. This claim should be researched thoroughly.

Review the Market

Since the Forex market is almost always open, every time you step away from the market, you must review what has occurred when you come back. This prevents you from making uninformed decisions based on partial information. For example, perhaps you believe the Japanese economy is on the rebound, which should cause the yen to strengthen against the U.S. dollar. You stop trading at 4 p.m. (the close of NYSE trading) on a weekday and turn off your computer.

In the meantime, Japan opens, and the government growth reports are released. They're negative, and the nikkei plunges. Although the yen remains stable, the markets believe that Japan has not turned the corner on its low economic growth. This belief could affect the yen's value. In addition, from a technical trading standpoint, tech indicators will still be generating signals with the passage of time—regardless of actual trading activity.

When you come back to your computer and prepare for trading, you should know this information. If you take the same expectation from the day before and view the market solely from the charts, you might miss the fact that the market sentiment has shifted. This could require a change in your strategy.

Market Manipulation

The predominant structure of retail Forex trading is based on a single market maker who provides traders with a two-sided price. This mechanism has inherent problems. During times of uncertainty or new information, the market can bounce quickly. This can cause *slippage,* which occurs when your execution price does not match your desired price. Although firms are taking precautions against this type of market pricing behavior, this will continue to be a major problem as long as traders have only a single choice of counterparties.

Traders should monitor price fluctuations leading up to an order execution. *Leaning,* which occurs when a market maker favors one side of the market to his own advantage, is unfortunately common in Forex. There is no proof that any particular market maker practices this behavior, but there are credible rumors, and traders have seen some strange price behavior that demands attention.

Manipulation of some kind unfortunately happens in every market, but in Forex it's almost a cottage industry because the structure of Forex makes it relatively easy. First, there is no true market, so even if the price on a trader's platform is at odds with other indicative prices, this doesn't mean that they are right and your market maker is wrong. Consequently, proving that you have been the victim of a lean is almost impossible. Second, in a single-market-maker system (typical of retail platforms), the trader is a captive client. He can either accept the market maker's pricing behavior or pack up his account and find another firm.

Just Because You're Not Paranoid Doesn't Mean They Aren't Out to Get You

It is commonly argued that Forex firms today would never resort to such dishonest activity. But unless there is direct regulation regarding pricing (and there isn't any yet), the hint of impropriety will be there. As long as dealers can see your positions while offering you prices, the temptation to price aggressively will be a problem.

However, the growth in the number of retail clients over the past few years has made this kind of behavior increasingly difficult to carry out. Firms now have thousands of clients watching currency movements, physically or with automation (API). This scrutiny has limited the flexibility market makers have over pricing. For example, if a market maker attempts a *stop sweep* (when a dealer artificially spikes the market to trigger stop orders), traders will be ready to *scalp* the dealer (trading on inefficiency between real and indicative prices). This can be so costly to the market maker that it's not worth it.

Leaning, however, can still occur. Here's how. Suppose a trader puts in a stop order at USD/CAN 1.4840. The trader's platform matches the indicative price (the secondary price feed, which is as close to the interbank rate as possible) at 1.4845/1.4850. It's close, but not there yet. Then the dealer gives a falling price over the platform feed even though the interbank price stays flat. When the price hits 1.484, the trader's stop order is executed, and the dealer buys. Now the dealer moves the price feed back into alignment with interbank prices and offsets the buy 1.4840 with an interbank sell 1.4845. The dealer has just made money—5 pips' worth. Remember, it is the market maker's objective to first make a profit and then an orderly market—regardless of what they claim.

Flatline Your Emotions

On some level, the highs and the lows are what trading is all about. It can be a rush when your strategy works and you make a successful trade. It's these emotions that keep you trading Forex and not investing your money in the safety of municipal bonds. But it is not advantageous for a trader to get emotional over a trade. It drains critical energy and distorts the decision-making process. A disciplined trader should understand all outcomes of a trade before it is entered, and there should be no real surprises. I know it's impossible to become a trade droid—and who would really want to? But the more a trader can control his emotions, the better he will become.

I worked with a trader who could never handle the anxiety of trading. Strangely, he was also the most disciplined trader I have ever met. He prepared every trade with meticulous analyses and carefully considered all possible results. But you could always tell how his trading was going simply by how he looked. When he was in a winning trade, he was well-dressed and clean-shaven. When he was losing, he looked like he had slept in his clothes. I told him to find a middle ground for his emotions, because at this rate he would burn out at an early age.

Trade with Your Personality

Over the past decade, behavioral researchers have examined the role that personal psychology plays in trading. Understanding some of the common mistakes traders make can better help you avoid these mental traps:

- **Self-confidence**—In trading, there is a very thin line between bravado and stupidity. A trader must be careful not to over-rate his or her abilities and knowledge. Traders should always review their strategy and search for alternative views and feedback.

- **Trade rationalization**—A major problem in Forex trading is the enormous amount of available information. Researchers have found that investors look for information that supports their trading views while ignoring or discounting evidence that runs counter to their position.

- **Information weighting**—When considering a strategy, a trader often gives greater weight to the first information he or she receives and then slants all additional information received after that.

- **Escalation of information weighting**—To justify past decisions, regardless of success, individuals continue to trade on previous strategies. To avoid this pitfall, a trader should view each trade as a unique action.

Filter Information

The Forex market is flooded with information. While in the U.S. equity market a trader has to deal with only a few economic indicators released every few days and national investment news, a Forex trader has to handle economic releases from all over the world, along with all the national and international news. A Forex trader must decide what is critical information and what is just noise.

That's easier said than done. Much of the filtering process fits in with the current trading environment. Back in the 1970s, interest rates played a critical role in currency movements. In the late 1990s, every economic indicator moved the market. From 2001-2004, after the shock of the September 11 attacks, geopolitical realities were the market mover.

Avoid Bias

Every trader brings preconceived notions to the market, but this is especially true in Forex. When you are dealing with nations, there is an unconscious labeling of the currency—almost a personification of the individual monetary units. Traders must be very careful not to bring this baggage into the markets. An example is the trading of the euro versus the U.S. dollar. In 2003, traders with a bias toward the U.S. dollar, who believed that the U.S. dollar should always be priced above the lowly euro, lost money quickly, selling euros and buying dollars as the euro continually strengthened.

A trader must view each currency as a trading vehicle and nothing more or less. Some people think selling the U.S. dollar weakens the U.S. This attitude, however, displays a profound ignorance of some basic macroeconomic theories.

10

What Moves the Markets: Basic Fundamental and Technical Trading Strategies

It seems that a major trend in Forex is to move away from the "dismal science" (economic fundamentals) to mathematics (technical). If you don't need calculators and the ability to quantify the movements, the reasoning goes, then don't bother. I think this is incorrect and misdirecting new traders. Debate between "tech" and "funds" is as old as trading and I'm not about to end it here. I do believe that certain currency pairs have a predisposition to act in technical patterns more than fundamental patterns, and vice versa. A rule of thumb is: Highly traded G7 pairs such as the EUR/USD and USD/JPY tend to move technically, while exotics tend to demonstrate strong fundamental behavior. In the end, however, my most successful models and corresponding trades are based on a blend of fundamentals, technical, and understanding of market sentiment.

Watch Your Fundamentals

When I first got into trading, I based my strategy on 100% fundamentals. To me, a currency was the equivalent of a nation's stock. Just as a company's stock usually drops when it reports lower-than-expected earnings, so will a country's currency fall if it shows, for example, weak economic growth. That's the theory. I thought if I could manage the fundamentals, I could predict where the nation's currency was going—and with that knowledge I would make winning trades.

I also thought the law of efficient markets would protect me. This law means that all important and relevant information about an investment is already known to investors, who use this information to determine an investment's true value.

In the foreign exchange market, I figured that any important new information about currency was developed by the government. And since governments protect their information (consider how secretive and cryptic Alan Greenspan is), I assumed I would have at least a 50/50 chance of picking an indicator direction correctly.

This, I thought, was also a good reason to go into Forex. In the equity markets, Morgan Stanley, and a host of other Wall Street insiders, get information before it is released to the general public. But in the Forex markets, only a few know what Greenspan will say before he says it. By trading on fundamentals I believed I had a chance to trade against any other player in the market, regardless of their size or position.

Then I learned that although Forex is efficient, the market mechanism is more complex and can offset many of the benefits.

Another factor is that all currency prices and values are relative, depending on how you look at it. A currency's position can be determined only by looking at another currency, and finding that exact relative price can be complicated. Since there really isn't any mathematical equation to determine the price of a currency— unlike in stocks—a currency's price is only a perception. This never-ending search is the cause of much volatility.

Still, I liked trading on fundamentals. As a history major in college, it made sense to me. There is a real underlying reason why a currency would fluctuate. I spent a lot of time studying Japan and predicting the economy's retreat into recession. I was convinced that the underlying nonperforming loans had ballooned to $500 billion and would put enormous pressure on Japan's monetary system. As it turned out, my predictions were correct. The yen in 2001 weakened from 110 to 130 against the U.S. dollar. Considering that I had forecast this result, you would think I would have made a hefty profit. But the yen didn't simply slide to 130 from 110 in a straight line. It was volatile, with sudden peaks and plunges. I had an enormous amount of money at risk—leveraged at 100 to 1. In hindsight I was overleveraged considering my timeframe.

This chapter provides a basic overview of fundamentals and technicals. I stress that before you place any money in the market, you should have complete and total understanding of all tools involved. Unfortunately, no book, analyst report, or $25-a-month signal service will tell you how and when to make trade. If you can't (or won't) put in the time to understand everything about what you will trade, you would be better off giving your money to a professional money manager. I have developed my personal trading strategy through years of trial and error. And even if I just explained it outright, I don't think it would be effective. Too many x- factors. Each strategy has a small but critical component of the individual trader—a behavioral aspect that fits the trader and makes him or her successful.

To be successful, take the information from this book and combine it with additional research and your personal strengths to create your own unique strategy.

Old Versus Fresh News

The above Japanese example illustrates the power of efficient markets. The law of efficient markets that work effectively in Forex had already priced all the information I had used in my analysis. But, while old news has already been priced into the market, that doesn't mean fresh news can't move the markets. And in the Forex market, these fundamental events will create price change. Fresh news is any unforeseen event that can't be factored into the current price In addition, there is fresh news in pre-scheduled events such as speeches, interviews, news conferences of key figures, and pre-scheduled economic releases. (see Figures 10.1 and 10.2).

An excellent example of fresh news hitting the markets was in the case of the EUR/USD in early Fall 2004. The eur/usd was stuck in at the 120–124 range until Alan Greenspan put a negative bias on the usd (during congressional testimony?) and the bears dug in. The eur/usd proceeded to move to the all-time highs of 135.

A breakout on fresh news can provide an excellent opportunity to trade. I have heard this strategy called a "news straddle," after the similar option play. The concept is that the nature of the event is unknown, but there will be a noticeable market reaction in either direction. Simply place two opposite trades around the current price. This is where the combination of technical and fundamentals are ideal. Technical should determine where you should place your orders, exits, and stops. Remember, fresh news will have the greatest impact on the market when the technicals are there to support the move.

The strategy is designed to capture temporary volatility as the market digests new information. I would only advise highly experienced and educated traders to attempt this strategy.

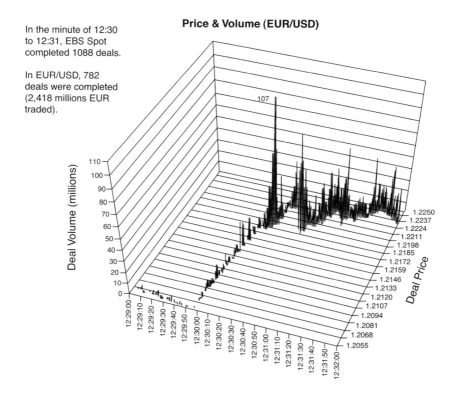

In the minute of 12:30 to 12:31, EBS Spot completed 1088 deals.

In EUR/USD, 782 deals were completed (2,418 millions EUR traded).

Price & Volume (EUR/USD)

Figure 10.1—A clear example of how fresh news moves the Forex market.[1]

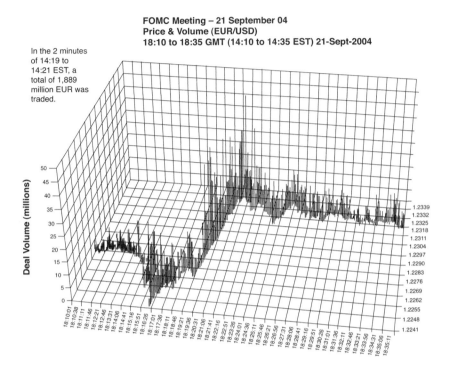

FOMC Meeting – 21 September 04
Price & Volume (EUR/USD)
18:10 to 18:35 GMT (14:10 to 14:35 EST) 21-Sept-2004

In the 2 minutes
of 14:19 to
14:21 EST, a
total of 1,889
million EUR was
traded.

Figure 10.2 — Fundamentals still move the Forex market.[2]

Market Movers

Even if you ultimately decide to trade on fundamentals, it's important to learn how various reports, announcements, and events move markets. These shouldn't be used as surefire guides for trading. After all, most macroeconomically-savvy investors already know how the market reacts in these situations, and markets have a tendency to act in unpredictable ways.

Fundamentalists believe that a currency is the product of a host of macroeconomic numbers, including growth rate, unemployment, budget deficits, inflation, trade deficits, and household debt, as well as the economy's government, stability, and policies.

While fundamentals have fallen out of favor in the Forex retail community, I still believe they play a critical role in accurate price discovery.

This chapter describes a number of factors that commonly affect a country's currency. Not one of these should be considered in isolation, however. They are all intertwined, and their impact depends on the local situation. An important fact to remember is that every Forex trade is made up of two currencies. This means that an event in one nation must be compared against the situation in another nation. Just because one economy is weakening doesn't mean all pairs with that currency will trade lower. It depends on how that weakening economy affects that country's situation—and currency.

Governments

Governments, for obvious reasons, have an enormous stake in what occurs in the foreign exchange markets. A currency is not just something people use to exchange goods; it is a symbol of national pride and power. One journalist compared it to a national flag. When a currency comes under pressure or is forced to be devalued, it can be humiliating to the government. It is an admission to the entire world of its own incompetence, impotence, or both. Governments that devalue often don't outlast the civil unrest they spark.

Governments have various tools at their disposal to control currencies. Many of them are ineffective, especially if the market has a strong opinion one way or the other about a currency's value. Still, governments often try to "talk up" (or down) a currency by stating their displeasure over the currency's value or by hinting at various measures they will take to move it. These statements can influence a currency, especially in the short term.

Other tools include the government's financial arm (in the U.S., it's the Treasury) and a nation's central banks. These institutions can do a number of things both short- and long-term that affect their nation's currency. These measures are explored in this chapter.

In more extreme cases, governments can take action that is akin to killing the patient to cure the disease. One is for a nation to default on its loans. Russia defaulted in 1998, and Argentina defaulted on $95 billion in 2001. Obviously, a loan default devastates the economy and destroys the country's credit-worthiness, possibly for decades.

Another tactic governments use is to impose strict controls on the money supply itself, which can include forbidding people from taking currency or other valuables out of the country. Malaysia, which was swept up in the same economic maelstrom as Russia, simply refused to allow foreigners to take their investments across the nation's borders. This draconian action did work in the short term, and the Malaysian economy stabilized, but the loss of confidence from investors has lasted much longer.

Important Currencies

There are hundreds of currencies in the world today, and dozens are available to be traded. Only a few currencies, however, make up the vast majority of trades. They are called the *majors,* and they include the U.S. dollar, the euro, the yen, the British pound, and the Swiss franc.

The U.S. Dollar

The U.S. dollar, despite not being immune to fluctuation, remains the cornerstone of the world economy. Oil is paid for in dollars, and virtually all foreign banks hold large dollar reserves as security. The dollar is the most heavily traded currency in the world. The size of the American government budget deficit and trade deficits put tremendous downward pressure on the dollar in 2003 and 2004.

The Euro

The euro, introduced as a physical currency in 2001, is used as money in 12 European countries and is the culmination of the dreams and ambitions of generations of statesmen. As a currency that represents more than 300 million people and some of the richest nations in the world, it is often openly discussed as the dollar's rival. Some people hope it will unseat the dollar's position as the world's reserve currency.

The Yen

Japan, the world's second-largest economy, uses yen for its currency. The Japanese government often intervenes to keep the yen at a favorable value and to ensure that Japanese exports remain competitive in world markets.

The British Pound

The pound, also called the sterling, is a popular haven outside the Eurozone. It usually gains if traders sense problems with the continental European economies. Some traders look for opportunities between gilts, British government gilt-edged securities, and the yield on the 10-year U.S. Treasury bill.

The Swiss Franc

The Swiss franc is traditionally a safe haven—a place investors rush to when there's global turmoil. The franc has climbed after stock market crashes and terrorist attacks. When a bomb killed the U.S. appointee to head the Iraqi Governing Council on May 17, 2004, the Swiss franc jumped 2 percent against the U.S. dollar.

Other Currencies: Exotics

As the world becomes more globalized, more and more currencies are available to be traded. I recommend that you do your research before investing in these currencies. The currencies that are actively traded tend to be safer, and you will most likely get tighter spreads, price disclosure, and price execution. However, currencies of lesser-known countries offer opportunities that should not be ignored. The following sections discuss some other currencies to keep an eye on.

The Yuan

The Chinese yuan, or remimbi, is pegged to the U.S. dollar. As China's economy grows more powerful, however, there is open speculation that the government will let the currency float freely. If this happens, the yuan will become a major player in world currency markets.

The Won

South Korea has emerged as a minor industrial powerhouse. Located between China and Japan, it is poised to play an even greater role in the Asian economic boom. The won, however, is still not easy to buy or sell.

The Real

Brazil's currency, the real, is open only to offshore counterparties, but it has floated since it was devalued in 1999.

The Rand

South Africa's currency, which floats against the other currencies, is a major secondary player in the currency market.

The G7

"G7" stands for "Group of 7," a club of the world's richest economies. The members are the U.S., Great Britain, Canada, France, Germany, Italy, and Japan. (It has also been called the "G8" to include Russia after the fall of the Soviet Union.) The organization first met in 1973 as the "G5," prompted by the collapse of the Bretton Woods Agreement, the first oil shocks, and a world recession.

Today, the world leaders of the G7 meet at least once a year, with lesser meetings of lower-echelon ministers occurring between the yearly meetings. For the most part, a G7 meeting provides photo opportunities of grinning world leaders and colorful flags sharing the same stage. That is usually about all that happens. Occasionally, however, the G7 acts together to influence currency levels, as they did in the mid-1980s. Emergency meetings of the G7, which usually are leaked to the press, are good indicators that some important action is being considered. A G7 meeting is also a good snapshot of the world's economic mood. In 1997, the G7 met in Denver, Colorado, where the U.S. economy was starting to roar ahead on the gains of the Internet boom. In a jovial mood, U.S. President Bill Clinton presented the other world leaders with cowboy boots. The other world leaders, who were leading struggling economies, were not amused. French President Jacques Chirac refused to try his on. At another meeting, in 2003, Europeans urged the U.S. to help boost the dollar, which had lost significant ground against the euro and was making Europe's exports more expensive in world markets. U.S. officials, however, publicly indicated that the dollar's level was fine, and the G7 meeting ended with no resolution on the disparity.

Central Banks

Every government in the world has a mechanism to control the supply of its currency. In most countries, it's a national bank, and these are key players in the currency markets. Each bank has a different reputation. Under Alan Greenspan's direction, the Fed reacts aggressively to changes in the economy. The Bank of Japan (BOJ) is known to frequently intervene with inconsistent results. The European Central Bank, although it has existed for only a few years, has resisted enormous political and public pressure to raise rates. It insists that its fundamental function is to keep inflation low, inspiring some to argue that the bank is fighting the last war and not the new one of high unemployment and low growth. Other national banks are considered little more than figureheads, without sound leadership or financial muscle to move the markets.

The U.S. Federal Reserve

The most closely watched central bank in the world today is the U.S. Federal Reserve. The Federal Reserve, also called the "Fed," was created in 1913 by Congress, which divided the country into

12 districts and established within each a District Federal Reserve Bank. These banks are overseen in Washington, D.C. by the Federal Reserve's Board of Governors, which has seven members appointed by the president to 14-year terms. The length of the term is intended to ensure stability and independence between presidents. The Chairman of the Board, however, is appointed by the president to a renewable four-year term.

The Fed's most important organization is the Federal Open Market Committee (FOMC), which, among other things, sets short-term interest rates. Each member of the Board of Members also serves on the FOMC, along with the president of the New York Reserve Bank and four other district bank presidents. The FOMC meets roughly once a month to discuss and review the economy and policy. Each member has one vote on setting economic policy.

Another Fed bank to watch closely is the New York Federal Reserve Bank, which is responsible for intervening in foreign exchange markets.

The European Central Bank

The Fed's counterpart in Europe is the European Central Bank (ECB). The highest decision-making body in the ECB is the Governing Council, which consists of the six members of the executive board and the 12 governors of the national banks. The Council, like its counterpart at the Fed, determines the interest rates banks are charged for obtaining currency from their national bank. And like the Fed, this number is closely watched.

The ECB executive board is appointed with the agreement of the 12 nations using the euro. The head official, akin to the Federal Reserve Chairman, is the president. The ECB works with banks that are closely tied to Europe (Great Britain, Denmark, and Sweden) but that don't use the euro. This umbrella organization of cooperation is called the Eurosystem. With the addition of 10 new members into the European Union in 2004, the monetary union is scheduled to expand into a market of 400 million.

The Bank of England

The Bank of England, the second-oldest national bank in the world, was founded in 1694. It started out as a place for the government to secure loans. It gradually expanded and became the "banker's bank" by providing credit to the nation's banking system. It was taken over by the government and "nationalized" in 1946. Since then, the bank has slowly regained its independence. It became operationally free of the government in 1997, especially to set interest rates. The Bank of England's Monetary Policy Board is comparable to the Fed's Open Market Committee. Today, the Bank of England also manages the UK's foreign exchange and gold reserves and the government's stock register.

The Bank of Japan

The Bank of Japan is directed by the Policy Board, which has nine members—a BOJ governor, two deputy governors, and six people chosen for their economic experience or expertise.

The International Monetary Fund

The International Monetary Fund (IMF) was founded as a part of the Bretton Woods Agreement in 1944. (The World Bank, the IMF's sister institution, was also founded at the conference.) The intent of the IMF's founders was to help avoid the destructive currency fluctuations in the period before World War II. At that time, each nation had devalued its currency in a bid to make its exports the most competitive. The result shattered economies and helped sow the unrest that flowered into Nazism.

Determined to avoid this ruinous competition, the conferees gave the IMF the responsibility of making sure member nations ran a stable exchange rate and balance of payments. If a country got into trouble, the IMF was there to provide a loan to avoid any wild destabilizations that could upset the global economy. The funds for these bailouts are provided by the member countries, and the size of their quota is mostly determined by the size of their economy and foreign reserves. The six largest quotas are the U.S., Great Britain, Japan, France, Germany, and Saudi Arabia.

Loans are called *tranches,* and they can be routine or emergency. Each country can borrow up to 100 percent of its quota. The first tranche is normally given with easy terms, but each succeeding tranche carries more qualifications. The IMF is like any creditor that provides loans—the larger the loan, the more control the creditor (in this case, the IMF) takes in its investment.

This has led to endless problems, because by the time a nation turns to the IMF, its economy is usually in shambles, its society is on the verge of revolt, and its alternatives are virtually zero. Although terms of the loans are hammered out in private, a nation's leader routinely blasts the IMF in public, blaming it for the economic turmoil the country is experiencing and especially the unpopular measures the government must implement as terms of the IMF's loan. IMF reforms typically call for higher interest rates and more balanced deficits—a recipe that slams the brakes on any economy and immediately increases unemployment in a society already plagued with unrest. During mass rallies against the IMF in Korea in 1998, for example, demonstrators in Korea held up signs that asked, "I aM Fired?"

This role has made the IMF a controversial institution in world politics. It attracts the ire (and stones and rotten vegetables) of protesters who see it as a pillar in a global economy based on injustice.

On the other hand, even supporters of the IMF almost always have some reason to criticize it—for lending too much money, for lending too little money, for being too strict, for being too lax, for being too early, for being too late. Others have argued that bailing out investors is subsidizing risky behavior.

In any case, currency investors should keep an eye out for the IMF. It is important to remember that the IMF is the fire engine sent to fight the fire. If the IMF shows up at a house, that means the house is burning down.

Private Financial Institutions

Banks perform several different roles in the currency markets. They are the middlemen for large transactions, handling large trades for corporate clients. Each of the large banks—CitiBank, JP Morgan, Goldman Sachs, HSBC—have departments where traders are given a pot of money and told to go make as much as possible. Some banks simply trade among themselves, using their expertise and resources to make speculative profits.

Corporations

Giant multinational corporations—Toyota, GE, BMW—are by default huge players in the currency markets. When an American buys a Japanese car or when a Japanese watches an American film, each purchase has to be translated back into the home country's currency and reported on that company's balance sheets. This makes corporations especially interested in currency fluctuations. Growth in revenues or profits could be flattened if a country's currency is falling.

Corporations can also influence currency fluctuations, when they put billions of dollars worth of currencies on the market to be bought or sold.

Another, less-known secret about corporations is that they are heavily involved in currency trading themselves. Some corporations today make as much money trading currency as they do selling their products.

Speculators

Speculators include everyone who jumps into the Forex market to make some money. They tend to operate under the radar. Hedge funds, individuals with large reserves of money, small investors, and traders all play the Forex market as a way to turn a quick trade into big profits.

Speculators are like the outlaws of the Wild West: They make their own rules. They are not interested in good or bad or how their investment affects individuals. They want to make money, and to do that they determine a currency's true value. They also trade a lot—up to 90 percent of the daily turnover is from speculators. In this sense they are vital to the market. With their relentless intensity, they keep the markets honest. Some writers compare speculators to Robin Hood, pulling down the elaborate veils of power and secrecy governments erect to protect themselves. If the Forex markets are a financial democracy, speculators are a powerful block of voters.

Since speculators are often behind the attacks that upset government plans, they are often singled out for abuse by public leaders.

Monetary Policy and Interest Rates

As mentioned, some central banks can lower or raise short-term interest rates in a bid to control the nation's money supply. In simple terms, lowering interest rates makes it cheaper to borrow money, thus stimulating consumption and economic growth. The run-up in auto sales and home prices in the U.S. in 2002 and 2003 was due mostly to Alan Greenspan's decision to lower interest rates six times, first in response to the stock market crash of April 2001 and then because of the terrorist attacks in September of that same year. Generally, the markets react favorably to cuts in interest rates and fearfully when rates are raised.

But there are several other factors to consider. Free credit expands the money supply and puts more dollars in wallets. With more dollars chasing goods and services, the law of supply and demand inevitably goes into effect. Prices rise and may spark inflation. If a currency is losing value through inflation, it will suffer in the currency markets. Consequently, raising rates can be greeted with relief, or it can be seen as too little, too late and confirm traders' fears that inflation is setting in.

Raising interest rates can also attract capital back into an economy, thus pushing up the value of a currency in the short term. If U.S. banks pay 1 percent interest for deposits, Great Britain pays 2 percent, and Europe pays 4 percent, investors will put their money in Europe, thus pushing up the euro.

That's why the words of the world's central bankers are examined with such intensity. Interest rates are vitally important to determining an economy's health. When they are moved, the markets react.

Inflation

The makers of economic policy fear few things as strongly as inflation. If inflation sets in, it affects everyone—corporations, suppliers, workers, employers, pensioners. Mostly, the effect is negative. The official tenet of most central banks is to keep inflation low. So if inflation is rising, as measured by the consumer price index (CPI) in the U.S., the Federal Reserve will most likely be forced to raise interest rates, which will cool economic growth. Investors are well aware of this relationship, making the monthly report of the CPI one of the most-watched numbers on Wall Street.

Gross Domestic Product

Every quarter, the government releases the percentage growth of the gross domestic product (GDP). The GDP is a broad measure of all economic activity in an economy. An advanced industrialized society such as Europe, Japan, or the U.S. prefers to see GDP growth between 3 and 5 percent. Anything lower indicates that the economy is in danger of stalling. Anything higher means the economy is heating up too fast and is in danger of inflation or a sudden crash. Developing countries can grow at much higher rates, but that has risks as well. China, for example, grew more than 8 percent in 2003 and broke 9 percent in the first quarter of 2004. Rather than please China's leaders, however, these red-hot numbers made them nervous. Too much growth and too much money can set up a country for a serious fall, as had happened in Thailand. To prevent this, Chinese leaders began tightening credit, which would reduce lending and cause the economy to cool, or experience a "soft landing," rather than crash.

Several other indicators, like the GDP, hint at economic growth. These include housing starts and retail sales. When both are high, it's genefrally considered a sign that the economy is doing well, but it may also prompt an interest rate hike.

(Un)Employment

Employment figures are an important indicator of an economy's health. A strong economy creates new jobs, thus providing employment for the hundreds of thousands of people who enter the workforce every year. However, if the economy is growing strong and there are more jobs than people to fill them, wages begin to rise as companies compete for the best workers. This can be great for individuals but bad for the economy. When wages rise too fast, so does inflation, which forces the central bank to raise rates and cool the economy. When that happens, the job market traditionally falls off.

On the other hand, a weak economy that creates no jobs spreads uncertainty and tends to tighten consumption. Without consumption, economic growth stagnates, but it may stimulate the Federal Reserve to loosen interest rates, thus leading to economic growth. That's why a higher unemployment number can actually stimulate the market, whereas a lower one can depress it. For example, throughout early 2004, the markets nervously watched for any sign that the Federal Reserve Chairman would raise interest rates. When unemployment numbers showed that jobs were being created—hence raising the probability of an interest rate increase—the markets actually fell.

The Beige Book

With so many numbers and statistics to keep up with, some investors simply direct their attention to a compilation of data called the "beige book." Released eight times a year, the beige book presents statistics from various government agencies about the U.S. economy, including manufacturing, real estate, home construction, consumer spending, employment, and wages. Using the beige book, investors try to get a firmer sense of where the U.S. economy is headed. The beige book is also the source most consulted by the Fed. If the beige book shows warning signs such as inflation or high unemployment, the Fed is more likely to act.

Government Spending and Taxes

Benjamin Franklin said that in this world nothing is certain but death and taxes. If a third thing could be added, it might be that governments will spend more money than they take in.

This is not necessarily a bad thing, especially in a recession. Money from the government is distributed through the social safety net (unemployment insurance, welfare, disability, social security), through contracts (usually for defense and security), and for emergencies (New York received several billion dollars after the

September 11 terrorist attacks). This extra money can help keep a bad situation from getting worse by arresting the downward spiral that causes economic depressions. Orders fall, so companies cut workers, who cut consumption. Orders fall again, forcing companies to cut still more workers, and so on and so on.

But government spending can also be an extremely inefficient way of allocating a nation's resources. In the U.S., congressmen routinely use "pork barrel" projects to reward favored constituents and ensure their reelection. In Southeast Asia, access to the government through relatives or other means meant that certain projects were favored over others. This allowed ill-conceived plans to go forward, with terrible consequences later. Observers called this system "crony capitalism."

A general rule of thumb is that capitalists like lower taxes, so the markets may react favorably to a party that takes power on a tax-relief platform. However, if the tax cuts appear reckless and dangerous, the markets will be wary.

Government Attitude

All politics is local, and a government's stability and attitude are essential to a currency's strength. Some leaders are antimarket and do things that may damage the country's standing in the international markets—although the moves may be popular in their own country. This can include defaulting on international loans, implementing expensive social policy, or erecting barriers to free trade.

The French are famous, or infamous, for their chauvinism. In a Europe where countries are supposed to set aside nationalism for the good of continental unity, chauvinism can be seen as a sign that economic reforms are being derailed. In 2004, the French drug company Aventis was in trouble and sought a merger partner. When Swiss pharmacy company Novartis showed interest, the

French government intervened. In no uncertain terms, the Swiss company was told to back off. In the end, another French company merged with Aventis, creating, as government representatives gushed, a "national champion." The French finance minister, Nicolas Sarkozy, was unapologetic.

"It is not a right of the state to help its industry," he said. "It is a duty." But this can scare off investors who prefer the markets to rule, not the government.

Equilibrium: "Parity"

Many different theories all roughly state that costs, services, and trade must be brought into balance. If they are not, the country's currency will rise or fall to find equilibrium. The *Economist* maintains what it calls the "Big Mac index." It compares the price of a Big Mac in dozens of different countries to determine if their currency is undervalued or overvalued. If a Big Mac costs $2 in New York and one euro in Paris, the currency exchange rate should be one euro = $2. If the currencies are being traded at $1.50 for one euro, the dollar is said to be overvalued and the euro undervalued. Eventually, according to this theory, the dollar will grow weaker and the euro stronger to make up this difference. This is also known as the "purchasing power parity" theory.

Trade Balance

One of the most relied-upon figures to calculate the value of a nation's currency is its trade balance. Nations that run regular trade deficits can expect to see their currency fall. The reason is simple: As the nation's currency flows overseas, it is reconverted. If more of a nation's currency is being sold than being bought, the law of supply and demand dictates that the currency will fall in value. The opposite is true for a nation that runs trade surpluses. The nation's currency is in demand, thus pushing up its value.

The effect of trade balance on a nation's currency, however, is never so clear-cut. A nation can run trade deficits if it continues to attract foreign capital for investment. For example, the U.S. ran trade deficits through most of the 1980s and 1990s. The dollar was propped up, however, because the U.S. attracted enormous amounts of capital. In short, everyone wanted a part of the booming American economy. The question market watchers ask is how long that can be maintained.

The J Curve Effect

This theory, illustrated in Figure 10.3, gained followers when the U.S. dollar lost significant value after 2002. The J curve says that in the short term a devaluation or depreciation of exchange rates might not improve exports and the current account deficit. In the first quarter of 2005, the U.S. dollar was at an unprecedented low but the trade deficit was hitting record highs. The balance of payments didn't reflect the rate change. The reason for this, according to the J curve effect, is the low price elasticity of demand for imports and exports. In simpler terms, most contracts have already been signed and can't take advantage of the new currency exchange rate. However, depreciation raises the amount of currency needed to purchase obligated imports, so in the initial period there is a slight increase in the trade deficit before the rebound.

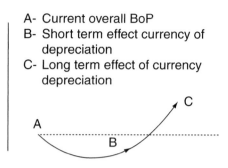

A- Current overall BoP
B- Short term effect currency of depreciation
C- Long term effect of currency depreciation

Figure 10.3—The J curve effect in action.

Political and Social Environment

The effect a country's political and social environment can have on its currency can be both simple and virtually impossible to recognize. But that effect should never be disregarded. A nation's economic policy can be broken into two categories. The first is monetary policy, which encompasses interest rates, money supply, and control over central bank activities. It also defines how much control a government exerts over its currency, called *managed currency*. The second category is fiscal policy, which is the government's attempt to direct the economy through taxation and spending.

A nation's social environment plays a critical role in the foreign exchange market and creates the greatest and most volatile risk. When social change occurs, it tends to be significant. Whether it's the velvet revolution in Prague, civil war in Sri Lanka, or a peace treaty in Northern Ireland, the event directly affects the foreign exchange market.

Governments generally follow three different policies toward foreign exchange rates:

- **Free float**—This is a foreign exchange system that lacks any government interventions and physical steering. It allows the market to adjust prices according to supply and demand. It gives officials the most flexibility to adjust to domestic policies and provides the smallest target for speculators.

- **Peg or "currency board"**—This is a foreign exchange system in which the domestic rate is fixed to a single foreign currency or a basket of currencies. A peg helps smaller nations and developing economies control inflation and provide stability, but it limits the government's economic flexibility and gives speculators an easy target.

- **Dirty float**—This system is a combination of free float and a peg. The currency's value is not a pure product of market forces because the nation's central bank occasionally intervenes. However, the currency is also not legally pegged to a specific exchange rate. The dirty float is arguably the most widespread system today. In 2003, for example, Japan intervened eight times to weaken the yen.

Currency Board or Peg

The popularity of currency boards comes and goes like a fashion fad. A peg can be very attractive because it can allow a nation to control inflation and develop a credible monetary policy by fixing its currency to a larger, more stable single currency or to a basket of currencies. Time after time, however, pegs prove unstable in the long run and are easy targets for foreign exchange speculators. A currency board or peg must have three elements: an exchange rate that is anchored to a single currency or a basket of currencies, convertibility, and long-term commitment to the monetary policy. This mechanism gives financial markets and the public the assurance that each unit of domestic currency is equally backed by an anchor currency of foreign reserves. A current example of an active peg is Argentina's one-to-one peg to the U.S. dollar. A peg can offer economic credibility, control inflation, and reduce financial costs. In addition, it can give the government the flexibility to lower interest rates and spur economic growth. But there are some significant downsides, especially in countries that try to cure their weak banking system and volatile economy with a peg. With a peg in place, a nation has limited use of fiscal and monetary policy. In addition, as the world learned the hard way in the Asian crisis, nations can become slaves to their foreign exchange policy.

One of the key lessons of currency pegs is that traders should respect a government's fiscal and monetary policy without overestimating how much control it truly has. In the U.S., for example, many economists agree that the president has very little, or no, power to effectively steer the economy. For example, the Republican Party has a reputation for being "business-friendly," while the Democratic Party supposedly is not. However, the U.S. economy has performed just as well under Democratic administrations since World War II as it has under Republican ones. The idea that presidents can wave a magic wand and conjure up economic growth is certainly false, but it is decidedly true that the economy and investors react to the actions of the president and other world leaders. Markets, after all, are the result of millions of decisions made by individuals, and individuals can get nervous or even panic.

Even during the economic boom times of the late 1990s, the markets reacted negatively when the lurid details of Bill Clinton's affair with intern Monica Lewinsky came to light. More serious was the August 1991 rumor that Mikhail Gorbachev had been kidnapped. The dollar spiked upward because the entire project of European integration would be threatened if Russia were to fall under the rule of a hostile dictator. The rumor proved false, and the dollar fell back to its previous trading levels.

Subjectivity

It would be a costly mistake to view fundamental trading as predictable—as if currency movements were a mechanical response to an action. This is simply not the case in Forex. Just because Great Britain's GDP increases and the U.S. GDP decreases doesn't mean that the GBP/USD will increase in value.

After all, the importance of information is subjective, depending on who is receiving and interpreting it. Since fundamentals are factual and transparent, all participants have an equal opportunity to analyze information. It's various interpretations of the same information that creates market volatility. Market psychology and behavior, predictions of fundamental changes, perceptions, and what data has already been discounted all become factors in fundamental trading. It is this complexity that throws off new Forex traders and drives them to become technical traders.

There are two distinct factions of traders: Technical analysts and chartists.

Technical Analysis

Technical traders have found a home in Forex. Some speculate that because of market efficacies and number of participants trading the major currencies, currencies move in very technical patterns. In addition, in a market where trades can last less than a minute, fundamentals might not give a trader the edge. Therefore, those who understand these patterns will have an advantage.

Technical traders don't base their strategies on fundamentals, which they believe are already reflected in a currency's price. Instead, technical traders study historical price movements. Utilizing those historical prices, they develop mathematical models or pattern recognition to predict future prices, and they use this information to take positions.

In this section, I have laid out the real basics of technical analysis that I use with some regularity. Traders looking to become more versed should find additional material. One great Web site is called www.stockcharts.com; while this site is targeted to stock traders, its information can be adapted to Forex (in technical trading the underlying vehicle becomes irrelevant).

Determining the Trend

The first task in technical trading is to determine the overall pattern of the market's broader movement—its *trend* (see Figure 10.4). This is most easily done by connecting two consistent points, such as a peak to a peak or a trough to a trough. This shows whether the market's trend is up or down. By connecting several of these points, a fuller picture emerges. Although the market might appear to be zigzagging, its true movement will be revealed. A trend can be established for various amounts of time—for minutes or for years.

Apart from uptrends and downtrends, a market can settle into a consolidation pattern, which essentially means that it isn't going firmly in one direction or the other. In all cases, the market creates points of support and resistance. Often, the market settles into familiar patterns.

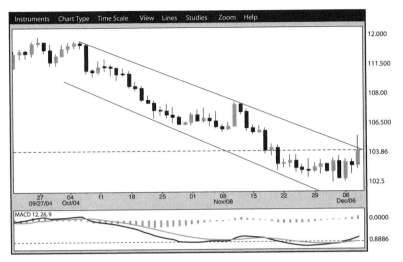

Figure 10.4—A basic downward trend in the USD/JPY.

Support and Resistance

These technical patterns, shown in Figure 10.5, play an important role in the Forex market and are used by almost every type of trader. *Support* is a price point below the current market price, where buying occurs to create a reversal to the downward trend. *Resistance* is a price point above the market price where selling pressure reverses the upward trend. Support has more buyers, and resistance has more sellers. Forex traders will find a lot of activity around these price points. Figure 10.6 is another example of upward and downward trends.

Note:

The trend and support and resistance are, in my mind, the most important technical indicators. They have moved away from just an illustration of historic price action into the realm of behavior finance, meaning a reflection of the trading habits of individual traders and market psyche en mass.

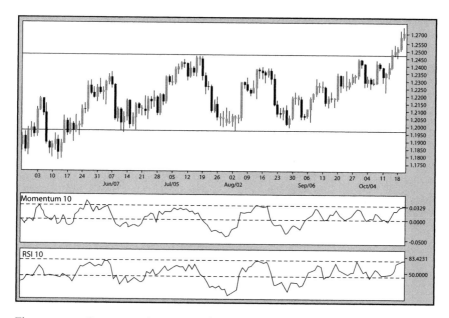

Figure 10.5—Support and resistance for the EUR/USD daily chart.

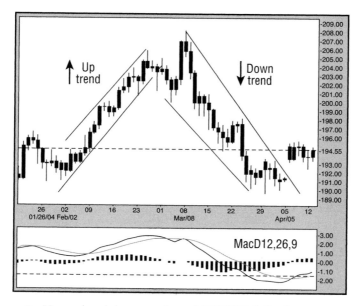

Figure 10.6—Upward and downward trend GBP/JPY daily chart. Notice the significant gap on April 5.

Chart Patterns

Markets follow certain patterns that have become well known to traders. Before we look at these patterns, here's one final reminder: Always be humble to the markets. Experts, geniuses, and madmen have all spent years trying to discern the pattern behind the blitz of numbers that represent market movements—a pattern that will allow them to predict market behavior with perfect accuracy and lead them to riches. Almost all have failed. Even those who do succeed do so only temporarily before the mood behind the markets shifts, leaving their elaborate models outdated and useless.

On the other hand, some investors are clearly better than others. Although some of that success may be due to instinct, it is also true that every successful investor has put in time to understand the markets and the trends that move them.

One of the most famous technical patterns is called head and shoulders. It happens when the market rises, then falls an equal amount, then rises again much higher than before, then falls again an equal amount, then rises and falls again in a shape almost the same as the first rise. On a graph, it looks like a small hill (the left shoulder), a large hill (the head), and a small hill again (the right shoulder), as shown in Figure 10.7.

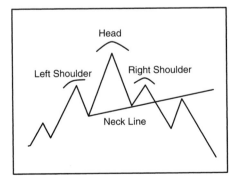

Figure 10.7—A head and shoulders pattern.

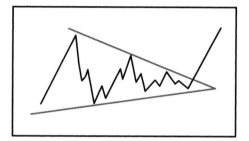

Figure 10.8—A symmetrical triangle breaking out in a bullish uptrend

Sometimes the triangle pattern favors the uptrend or down-trend, in which case it can become a *descending* or *ascending right-angle triangle*. In the descending triangle, the line drawn between the troughs is flat rather than rising, which indicates that the declines are deeper than the gains.

Why does this happen? When the price drops, buyers sense that it is oversold. They enter the market, pushing the price back up. Sellers see the gain and take profits, pushing the shares back down. The price falls, buyers reenter the market, and sellers sell again. The overall volume favors the sellers, and the price trends down-ward. Finally, the buyers decide that the price is unjustified, and they sell as well, causing the price to fall through the floor. This indicates that the market is in a bearish phase. In a bullish phase, the trend is the opposite, with the breakout being through the point of resistance.

The *wedge* pattern is similar to the symmetrical triangle. The trend lines of the highs and lows come together at an angle. Usually, this angle points up or down, showing whether the market is in a bullish or bearish trend.

The *channel* pattern is marked by indecision but usually does not buck the larger trend. The lines from peak to peak and trough to trough generally run flat on light volume.

The *flags and pennants* pattern is also a period of indecision, usually right after a big move in the currency. More often than not, the currency basically pauses at a flags and pennants pattern and then resumes whatever direction it was going before. The trend lines for the peaks and troughs run parallel.

An alternative to the standard price charting styles is the *candlestick* chart, which was developed by the Japanese in the 1700s to chart rice trading. Just like a standard bar chart, it shows the highs, lows, open, and close over a designated period of time. It uses a solid or empty body to illustrate whether the time frame is up or down. If nothing else, the effect is dramatic and illuminating. This kind of chart has many patterns, with intriguing names such as dark cloud cover, Gravestone doji, and three black crows. Although the validity of the patterns' predictive ability is questionable, one thing is for sure: A trader needs to be able to control his or her emotions. The chart effect can panic undisciplined traders. Figures 10.5 and 10.6, shown earlier, are examples of candlestick charts.

Fibonacci Pattern

In the eleventh century, an Italian mathematician named Leonardo Fibonacci noticed a pattern resulted when he added a series of consecutive numbers:

1 + 2 = 3

2 + 3 = 5

3 + 5 = 8

5 + 8 = 13

8 + 13 = 21

Each number in the sequence—3, 5, 8, 13, 21—results in the next number when it is multiplied by 1.618. This ratio appears in patterns across nature—from the structure of honeybee cells to musical notes—and has been called the Golden Ratio. Traders use Fibonacci's number to determine retracement from a current price. Important retracement levels are 38.2 percent, 50 percent, and 61.8 percent.

Elliot Wave Theory

This is a complex theory that predicts future price movement through the study of wave patterns. The critical aspect of this theory is its determination of the individual waves' relativity to the greater wave structure. There are two major types of waves: those that move with the trend, called *impulse waves,* and those that move against the trend, called *corrective waves.* Impulse and corrective waves can be dissected further. This theory relies on the fact that waves move in patterns. As soon as you have identified the wave classification, you can predict the next price movement.

Gann Angles

This is perhaps one of the chartist's most obscure tools. The Gann Angles theory is based on W.D. Gann's (1878–1955) trading writings. This mystic's art depends on angles, based on time and price intervals. In broad terminology, the "perfect" angle is 45 degrees, known as the 1×1 trend line. The angle forms support and resistance lines. In every price movement, a fan of angles is created. When the lines are broken, the next likeliest support and resistance is the next angle. You must have some faith in charts to trade on this theory, although some traders swear by it.

Andrews Pitchfork

This is a derivative of the classic support and resistance theory. It consists of three parallel lines (points you select) that follow the trend. After you have picked your three points, this theory functions much like support and resistance. The key is picking the right points. Traders generally choose a major peak or trough and then two other points along the chart to create support or resistance. The middle line of the pitchfork is drawn from the selected peak to the midpoint of the other points and is drawn parallel and at the same angle.

Indicators 101

Moving Average

In its simplest form, the moving average is just the average of historical prices, indicating potential momentum. This illustrates the historical trend by "smoothing" volatility. The trader can choose a time frame according to his or her preference. The longer the time frame, the smoother and less sensitive to price change the moving average becomes. And the shorter the time frame the more sensitive to price change and therefore subject to whipsaws.

Moving Average Convergence/Divergence (MACD)

This is a popular oscillator. It is created by defining two weighted moving averages, a 12 day and 26 day exponential moving average, and deriving the difference between the two. This difference forms a MACD line—a horizontal trigger line. When two moving averages cross below the trigger line, which is usually a nine-day EMA, it is considered a bearish signal. When the moving averages cross above the line, it is considered bullish.

Relative Strength Index (RSI)

This is a momentum oscillator that measures degrees of upward pressure against downward pressure. The ratio is then normalized into a scale that runs from 1 to 100. When the RSI registers above 70, it's considered a sell signal—the currency is overbought. When the RSI reads below 30, it is a buy signal, and the currency is viewed as oversold.

Stochastic Oscillator

This is a momentum indicator that compares a currency's closing price relative to its price range over a specific period of time. This indicator is based on a theory that states that in an uptrend prices tend to close near the highs and in a downtrend they close near the lows. In addition, as the trend matures, the opposite begins to occur, signaling a reversal. In a mature uptrend, prices close near the low, and in a downtrend, they close near the high.

Bollinger Bands (BB)

This is an excellent measure and illustration of volatility. In simple terms, the Bollinger Bands are two lines charted two standard deviations away from the moving average. BB adjusts to market conditions, widening during times of volatility and tightening during calm. Often the lines are shown with lines between the two, which represent the moving average. The trader's choice of the moving average time frame varies but tends to be about 10 days for short term, 20 days for intermediate, and 50 days for long term. Bollinger Bands don't generate trade signals by themselves.

Figure 10.9 demonstrates the concepts of MACD, RSI, and BB.

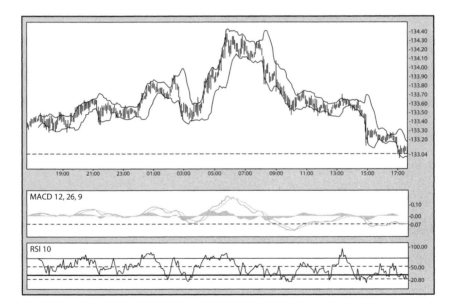

Figure 10.9—Looking for a signal in the EUR/JPY 5 minute using Bollinger Bands, MACD, and RSI.

Parabolic Stop and Reversal (SAR)

This is a good indicator of points to set trailing stops. The SAR is based on very complex mathematical models, but it basically considers price movements. There are two variables—the step and the maximum step. The higher the step, the more sensitive SAR is to price movements. The maximum step controls the adjustment of SAR to price movement. The inventor of the indicator suggests setting the step to .02 and the maximum step to .2. In addition, this indicator is very effective during periods of trend.

Average Directional Index (ADX)

An excellent indicator developed by Welles Wilders, the ADX is used to measure a trend's strength and integrity. As with most indicators, it is based on difficult math but is relatively easy to use. ADX doesn't give bullish or bearish signals, only a reading from 0 to 100 that gauges the trend's strength. A number above 50 indicates a strong trend and below 20 a weak trend. By combining the ADX with the positive (+DMI) and negative (–DMI) directional indicators, you have a complete and powerful trading system for Forex.

Starter Technical Model

As amazed as I am at how many traders look for the magic model, system, or signal that will explain the markets, I am also stunned by the amount of experts willing to sell them their voodoo snake oil. First, I have said all along that traders need to build their own personal trading strategies; there are no "off-the-shelf" solutions. Second, I don't want my explanation of Forex to be lumped in with all the other get-rich-quick charlatans. That said, I know what it was like to look at a Forex screen and have no trading clarity. In the next sections, I will explain a basic trading strategy for scalping. This technique is well-known throughout the trading communities. It is not very complex or complicated, but good systems don't have to be. It will, however, provide a new Forex trader with the basic building blocks to begin developing their own trading systems. I believe that, with a few minor adjustments, this system can become profitable.

Early in my career, I worked with an Elliot Wave specialist and, after many losing systems, he convinced me that this was the best approach to the Forex market. So, I hit the books and studied and—before I was completely ready—began trading on this indicator. Let me rephrase: I traded over his shoulder, but I never really felt 100% confident about the rationale behind the system. I believe this happens to many new Forex traders. They search for a trading system and blindly execute trades on partial information and understanding. I'm sure you have guessed how this story ends. Whenever a trade would develop, I would look for confirmation from the guru—he would say it looked good and by the numbers they were good trades. But, I could never find traction with this model. More were losing bets than successful ones, but he would hit winning trade after winning trade. The difference (of course) was that, while utilizing the Elliot Wave method, he had developed his own unique system in which he was comfortable and understood the rationale behind the trade. Me? I was just trading blind.

Memorizing a formula might provide a few profitable trades, but it will never allow you to become successful in the long run. A trader must understand the philosophy of why a strategy works (or doesn't) so they can recognize faults and correct them. If you are using a weighted moving average and the signals are coming fast, you will need to know how to adjust the weighting or timeframe to filter false signals (i.e., noise).

Scalping

I really enjoy this strategy and believe it is perfect for Forex trading. A skilled, aware, and disciplined trader can make a decent profit scalping (dealers, by the way, hate them). In addition, a scalping strategy is also ideal for an automated trading system, which will have a faster recognition and execution than a manual trader. A word of caution: While this strategy sounds appealing, it takes an experienced trader to do it successfully. The scalping technique is as old as trading itself and has its roots on the physical trading floors and in cross exchange arbitrage. Today's retail Forex traders have the ability to view multiple price feeds on the same vehicle, similar to the separated exchanges in days of old. This fragmentation can gives scalpers a slight edge on hesitant dealers.

Scalping is the rapid entry and exists in trades that are geared to take small bites from a larger move.

The spreads must be tight: two to three pips are the best and don't bother with anything over five pips. In addition, you should have a few different price streams for comparison. Also, most retail prices are made by individuals on a dealing desk, which have unique tendencies. After watching prices long enough, you will be able to see patterns in price behaviors. And, sometimes, they can give you insight into the firm's dealing strategy.

Trade size should be half or even one-third of what you think you should trade. Remember this is a training model, so you will need room to make mistakes.

Stick to the majors for higher liquidity, more orderly, and tighter spreads.

Risk reward ratio is 2:1. If you're looking to capture 20 pips, risk 10 pips.

Never let a winning trade turn into a loser. Always take profits, even if it's just one pip. This is not about capturing the big move (that's another strategy). There will be many more signals.

Always stick to your stops. If you don't, you will see a week's worth of grueling work wiped out in seconds. Small losses can become huge for traders who just can't let go. Mentally, you must be prepared to lose almost as much as you win.

This is the most intense type of trading. A trader must be committed to the strategy. There is no leaving the screen when it looks like a trade is coming into play. A trader must be ready to pull the trigger when the opportunity arrives.

I use simple two-weighted moving averages.

The first set to wma 5 period and second to wma 20 period. I'm looking for short time frames: Five-, fifteen-, and thirty-minute bid charts. Then, the wma's cross to enter the market in the direction of the last bar.

It's critical to see the wma cross. Don't jump prematurely, no matter how tempting it is.

Since wma are lagging indicators, there are times when fast-moving markets leave scalpers in the dust. If the last bar is large, say 10-15 pips or greater, then stay away from the trade. Otherwise, you will only catch the retracement.

Stay away from slow moving, thinly traded times (depending on currency pairs, late NY early Asia). This period will send lots of false signals.

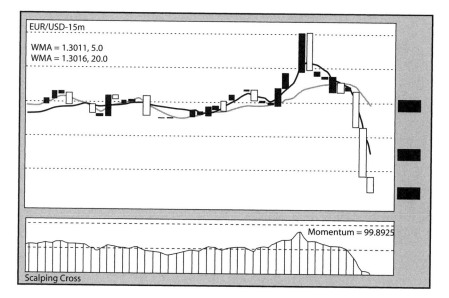

Figure 10.10—Scalping at European open. Notice the false signals during the thinly traded Asian market. Scalpers must be particularly aware of time-based indicators because they will constantly generate signals—regardless of actual volume. Once real trading begins in Europe, the WMA cross sends a strong signal.

Technical or Fundamental?

Currently, I am a 60% technical 40% fundamental trader. However, I don't automatically recommend this trading blend for every investor. It depends on what kind of trading best suits your strengths. And never forget, it's as important to stick with your strategy and learn from your mistakes as it is to pick a winning strategy.

Let me close this chapter with a story about another critical lesson—the importance of being humble.

I still remember my last fully fundamental trade. Like anyone who's spent time in a casino, you might remember your big wins, but it's the losers that stay with you forever. I have to admit I was looking for a good trade. Worse, I needed one. In 2001 the U.S. GDP numbers were dismal— –.3 percent compared to 4.1 percent in 1999 and 3.8 percent in 2000. The U.S. economy was officially in a recession for a portion of 2001.

In spring 2002 the first quarter's economic numbers were about to come out, and I felt they would really move the markets. Any number—good or bad—would cause a strong move. Investors were nervous, wondering where the U.S. economy was going. The economists from major financial firms had mixed forecasts.

I wasn't rooting for a number one way or the other, even though I'm an American and want my country to prosper. I had one side of the trade, which was the USD, the motive GDP. I needed the other side of the currency trade. The dollar could gain strength against one currency and lose value against another. Sometimes the hardest part of a trade is figuring out what currency will be affected in the counterreaction. That was certainly true at the start of 2002. At the time the Europeans had just launched the euro, and there was a definite feeling in the markets of America versus Europe. Lines were clearly drawn in currency trading worldwide. When U.S. markets dropped, the assumed benefactor was Europe. There was also lots of talk about the euro becoming the world's dominant currency and Europe the new economic ruler. On the other side, European Union bears believed the currency would fall apart because the EU was weak and unstable and that the U.S. would regain its rightful place as soon as the aftermath of the tech bubble resolved itself.

My trade was euros for dollars. I planned to hold the currency for 5 to 10 minutes, and I would be out.

Then the GDP number came out at 6.8 percent! This was a huge number for a developed nation and especially for the U.S. The dollar roared back as I began to sell euros for dollars. The price moved slightly in my favor and then headed straight down. I effortlessly went through my stops before it settled right underneath.

Later that day, after I had bailed out of my positions, the market headed in my direction. To me it seemed to be just in spite, but that's how the Forex market goes.

Endnotes

1. Source: EBS.
2. Ibid.

11

BLACK SWANS AND
ROGUE TRADERS

No market or investment is a sure thing. Foreign exchange investors must be especially careful, because the Forex market can be blindsided from many different directions. Nothing in the Forex market is "unthinkable." A terrorist attack, an upset in an election, or an off-the-cuff comment from a government official can set off a storm of speculation and trading. Or perhaps a government simply does something everyone assumed was impossible—a devaluation or an intervention. These events are "black swans," which represent something utterly surprising and unusual.

The Inherent Instability in the Forex Market

Swings in currency value always seem obvious in hindsight, but those caught up in them almost never know exactly when, or how much, a currency will move. That is because the "X factor"—the element of the unexpected that is present in all markets—is far more potent in the foreign exchange market.

Clive Crook, in the *Economist* (May 2, 2003), explains why. It is conventional wisdom that increased trade in goods and services is beneficial because it offers consumers more choices. Americans, for example, can match their tastes and preferences to a wide variety of automobiles, mostly because of open trade. The Forex market is good for the same reason—it offers people more choices. They can also invest in currencies from around the world, each with different strengths and weaknesses. But, as Crook darkly notes, the increase in the number of choices also increases the chances that the investor will make a bad investment. And whereas most people can tell a well-made car from one of poor quality, currencies are far more difficult to understand and judge.

For one thing, investors are less able to make an intelligent decision about something in a foreign business culture than about something that is near and familiar. Hence, investing in foreign capital raises the odds that investors will make less-sound selections.

This would not be as serious if investors were stung only when markets went down and investments went sour. Yet dramatic currency swings are rarely so kind. They can quickly spill into surrounding financial sectors and trigger a series of falling dominoes of failed institutions—companies, funds, banks, central banks, and governments. Individuals, who may have no interest in or understanding of the foreign exchange market, can ultimately be just as devastated as the investors.

Crook writes about why investor ignorance of the forces behind currency movement compounds the likelihood of a destabilizing crash. "Investors tend to deal with uncertainty in ways that aggravate the problem. If information about underlying value is absent or obscure, they are likely to become preoccupied with the views of other investors."

This isn't necessarily a bad thing, observes Crook, because one investor can learn something important that is spread quickly to the rest of the investing community. But "now and then, it degenerates into crowd hysteria."

Several times in history, investors have acted more like sheep than investors who respect reality, and not just in the Forex markets. The stock bubble of the late 1990s is a good example, when seasoned market watchers such as Warren Buffet withdrew in disgust from the markets because the valuations were so out of line with earnings.

Because it is difficult for investors to understand what conditions are like in another part of the world, the global currency market is therefore prone to these wild, speculative swings.

Another factor, however, makes the currency markets even more susceptible to swings—leverage. Through leverage, as you have read, an investor with modest assets can draw on enormous sums to invest in the foreign currency market, thus making an oversized impact. I have strongly recommended that the average investor avoid this temptation. Through leverage, it may be possible to win big, but it is also possible to lose even bigger.

These losses wipe out the individual investor, but they also affect the various lenders who loaned the investor the money in the first place, who often didn't fully understand the risk they were taking on. Thus, financial institutions can suddenly melt away after the disastrous trades of one dealer.

The Tequila Crisis

One of the first surprise collapses of a currency in modern foreign exchange history occurred in 1994 in Mexico. At the beginning of that year, no one predicted or expected what was about to happen. After all, the North American Free Trade Agreement (NAFTA) had passed, uniting Mexico, the U.S., and Canada in a free-trade block. Trade was flowing, and people expected the benefits of free trade, because everyone had assumed it would be enormous.

Moreover, after decades of walling itself against the "Yankee colossus," the Mexican government was doing economically, as one academic called it, right. The government budget was balanced, companies were being privatized, and tariffs were being lowered. The IMF gave a "strong and unqualified endorsement of Mexico's economic management." (Incidentally, there is an open secret among Wall Street analysts. To determine which country's economy will implode next in riots and unrest, simply look to see where IMF agents have been most active.)

Yet in early 1994, Mexico's finance minister, Guillermo Ortiz, told the Chamber of Deputies in Mexico City that the peso should be devalued, and that this idea had the support of international financial institutions. There were other signs of trouble. A bitter and dirty election brought fears of government instability. An armed rebellion brewed and then exploded in Chiapas, and a familiar political figure was assassinated.

Against this backdrop, investors began exchanging pesos for dollars in rapid amounts and pulling their money out of the country. The bank of Mexico faithfully exchanged the currency until it ran out in December 1994. The government then announced a devaluation, pulling the peso off its peg with the dollar. The lesson here is that it is almost impossible to control a devaluation after it begins. The market has a mind of its own, as the Mexican government soon found out. Originally, the government wanted a 20 percent devaluation to restore the competitiveness of its exports against U.S. imports. In a sudden, terrifying few weeks, the peso plunged more than 50 percent, destroying pensions and savings and slamming the economy to a halt. GDP melted 9.6 percent in the third quarter year-over-year between 1994 and 1995.

If this story of economic collapse surprised speculators, the next move probably did even more so. The U.S. government, in an unprecedented move and in the teeth of public griping, bailed out Mexico with a $50 billion loan.

Surprisingly, the bailout worked. The Mexican economy was hobbled but not wrecked. It soon resumed positive growth, but the lessons of Mexico's flirtation with disaster apparently were not learned.

The Asian Crisis

Consider Thailand in 1997. The economy, one of the so-called "Asian tigers," had been growing at more than 8 percent a year, giving the nation an air of hope, satisfaction, and strong development. Skyscrapers were being built and golf courses laid out, and a rising middle class was eagerly spending baht—the nation's currency—for luxury goods and automobiles. Property values rose rapidly.

Thais were confident that they could mirror the success of Japan, an Asian power that had gone from the ruin of war to the world's creditor nation in four decades.

The euphoria, however, masked growing problems. Investor money had poured into the country, but much of it was spent on ill-conceived projects or frittered away in corrupt bargains or bribes. Skyscrapers were built with little thought about who would eventually inhabit them. Real estate was profitable for those inside the country, but it could not be easily converted into a form that could be traded overseas.

Making Thailand far more vulnerable was the fact that the baht was rigidly tied to the dollar. In 1995, the Thai economy started to feel the strain. There was a dip in the semiconductor business, which was a major Thai export, and growing competition from China hurt the sale of Thai goods. The real estate market became saturated. Prices fell, and the banks that depended on those loans saw their defaults rise rapidly.

Worse, the dollar began to appreciate rapidly after 1995, pulling the baht up with it. The Thai economy was suddenly made much less competitive compared to its Asian neighbors. The trade balance swung.

Under these pressures, Thai financial institutions began to collapse. The government promised a bailout, but it didn't have the resources to come through. Within months, the Thai central bank ran through $28 billion of its $30 billion reserve.

Panicked investors pulled their money out of the country. Currency speculators began to attack the currency by selling baht for dollars. With no reserves left, the Thai central bank surrendered. On July 2, 1997, Thailand bowed to the inevitable and let the baht float against the dollar. The currency quickly fell 15 to 20 percent and by the end of the year had lost half its value. It was the lowest exchange rate for the baht since Thailand began keeping records in 1969. The lower exchange rate made Thailand's debts to foreign investors suddenly balloon to $70 billion.

This was not the end of the crisis. With the Thai baht devalued, the nation's neighboring countries, which also relied on exports, suddenly found themselves unable to compete against Thai products. Southeast Asian stock markets fell 35 percent. These countries were pressured to devalue as well, and Indonesia and the Philippines followed.

In Malaysia, Premier Mahathir bin Mohamad had poured investors' money into erecting the tallest building in the world, the tallest control tower in the world, and the tallest flagpole in the world. Now, these poor investments came back to haunt him as the country's currency crashed. Rattled by this sudden change in fortune, he begged Malaysians to travel abroad, pawn their jewelry, and return to Malaysia with the currencies to deposit in the local bank.

Mohamad, like so many other world leaders when confronted with an economic crisis, found scapegoats.

"All these countries have spent 40 years to try to build up their economies and a moron like Soros comes along," he said, referring to the billionaire currency speculator George Soros.

The contagion spread to Korea. Korea was no small economy, but an export powerhouse that had built itself over four decades into the world's 11th largest economy. Nonetheless, the Korean wan faltered and then collapsed under the pressure, and the Korean government was forced to go to the IMF for a humiliating handout. Eventually, they received the largest bailout in IMF history—$57 billion.

This did not clear up the worries, and pressure on Korea intensified. The danger was that the fire would spread to Japan, the world's second-largest economy but one hobbled by low growth, a stock market collapse in 1989, and an inefficient banking system that propped up billions in bad loans. Japan, it seemed, was teetering. If that domino fell, there was only one more to go—the United States.

Fortunately, this didn't happen. The financial panic flared and burned out, and the relief was palpable from Tokyo to Washington to London. In New York, however, a lesson had been learned. The global economy was not just in word only. The traders of New York may never have heard of the baht or the Thai SET before then, but they knew it now, and they would never forget the fear as an economic tsunami rolled out of East Asia and threatened to breach America's shores.

Another important lesson of the currency panic of 1997 was the enormous impact this market could have on ordinary people. In Indonesia, Suharto had ruled for 32 years. Students, who had agitated for more democracy for years, burst into the streets in violent protest. The demonstrations shook Indonesian society and its rulers.

These are just a few examples of how the currency market has acted dramatically in the past and will most likely again sometime in the future. But the foreign exchange investor would be well advised not to prepare for the next catastrophe to make money.

Breaking the Bank of England

Currency meltdowns don't hit just poor or developing countries. They can rock the wealthiest and most powerful governments in the world, and they provide vivid examples of what happens when even a strong government with resources battles the will of the markets.

Consider the history of the European Union. As preparation for eventual monetary union and to prevent ruinous swings in currency value, the nations of Europe entered into an agreement called the European Monetary's System's Exchange Rate Mechanism (ERM). Under the ERM, Europe's currencies were weighted to the region's most powerful currency—the German mark. No currency was allowed to fluctuate more than 2.5 percent in either direction.

This was not solely a monetary agreement. European bureaucrats and leaders had spent 50 years building an architecture that would knit Europe together, making the horrific conflicts of the first half of the century no longer possible. During this time many of Europe's cities, especially in the center of the continent, had been bombed into shattered piles of rubble and singed wood. Most families had lost someone in battle. Helmut Kohl, chancellor of Germany during the 1980s, reportedly wept during a meeting with French president Francois Mitterand, saying he didn't want his son to die in another world war.

Such an ambitious project inspired grand visions among Europe's leaders, who spoke of building a new social and economic order. The project was by no means assured, and at several key junctures, Europe's leaders had signed agreements or made treaties in the full knowledge that their own people would reject them if the subject were placed before them in a referendum. Under this pressure, the leaders who were uniting Europe were often extremely defensive about any criticism of the project, and they regarded the actions of the market as detestable, as a bunch of barbarians who were trying to ruin their dream of a better and more peaceful world.

This would be especially true in 1993, when foreign currency speculators taught them a lesson they would never forget.

The problem with the ERM appeared in the late 1980s. In 1989, the Berlin Wall fell, and the Soviet Union collapsed soon afterward. Flush with joy over unification, West Germany pledged to absorb East Germany, with its masses of the unemployed, its fouled environment, and its obsolete factories.

This project would be enormously expensive, and to pay for it the Germans planned to hike their interest rates to attract capital and keep down the threat of inflation. This was fine for Germany, but the other countries of Europe, which had their currencies pegged to the mark, would have to raise their interest rates to keep pace, regardless of the state of their economies.

The high interest rates attracted a flood of capital to Europe. Normally, such an imbalance might cause investors to be wary, but in this case the governments had promised that they would maintain their currency's value—no matter what.

So the money kept coming in, and pressure began to build. High interest rates were all right in Germany, but elsewhere they were crushing growth. Unemployment figures kept rising, and any government that intended to stay in power would have to adjust or face the wrath of voters. Many citizens realized that economic union would be somewhat painful but ultimately worth it, but their patience was wearing thin.

It finally wore out in June 1992, when Danish citizens voted "no" to the question of joining the European Union. This result sent shock waves through political and economic circles and made the entire European project suddenly appear very fragile. The investors who had poured money into Europe began to suspect that something might be wrong and that the government pledges to keep their currencies strong might be unsustainable.

Large corporations, in a bid to hedge themselves, began dumping their European currencies for the mark. This practice spread to hedge funds, banks, and individual investors. The only organizations that appeared to be buying these currencies were the central banks of each nation, and these banks appeared to be running out of marks. If the vaults went dry, the banks would have no other choice but to allow their currencies to float. Sensing the incompatibility between government resources and economic realities, the speculators began to attack the currencies.

The first to fall was the British pound. Speculators borrowed pounds and began selling them for marks. Since no one else would pay such a high amount for marks but the government, the central bank was forced to honor the exchange at the official rate. The speculators kept selling pounds for marks, eventually draining the central banks of all marks. The English central bank borrowed $14.5 billion worth of marks and openly pledged to defend their currency. That amount lasted only days.

The last tactic available to the governments was to raise interest rates, making it too expensive for speculators to borrow. But speculators still figured to make a hefty profit as long as the pound was devalued, so they kept borrowing. In the meantime, the high interest rates slammed the brakes on the economy, pushing up unemployment and making economic life miserable. No government could survive this for long. The choice for Britain's leaders was a return to economic normalcy or the maintenance of their relationship with Europe. In the end, it wasn't a choice at all, and Great Britain officially left the ERM and let the pound float.

Many speculators got rich. George Soros, a wealthy hedge fund director who was among the speculators, pocketed $1 billion alone. After such an unprecedented humiliation at one of the most prestigious financial institutions in the world, press speculation focused on him. Since then, Soros has been known as "the man who broke the Bank of England."

Italy was next, and speculators used the same tactics to shatter the lira as they had humbled the pound. Italy dropped out of the ERM.

Other countries, sensing the growing panic, took extreme measures. Sweden raised interest rates to 500 percent. The Bank of Ireland raised them to 300 percent. Again, speculators could absorb the high costs because they knew the governments could never keep such rates in place for long. The result would be economic chaos.

Exhausted, Sweden and Ireland allowed their currency to float. Only France held out, fighting proudly against three successive speculative attacks. Finally, in August, the French central bank surrendered, and the franc was allowed to float. The ERM had been eviscerated.

Public officials, furious and humiliated, turned their rage on the speculators. One of them answered, "The thing you have to remember about bureaucrats and governments is that what they'd really like is for everyone to go away and just let them do whatever the hell they like and be answerable to no one and sit on a big pedestal and announce to the little people below what's happening in the world. When the people would sit up and say that's nonsense, you guys are wrecking the economy, they get upset. People are questioning their actions, and they don't like it." (Millman, 64)

Interventions

Government interventions come in all sizes and are launched for various reasons, but they all share one unifying characteristic—they ultimately fail if they are contrary to the long-term trend moving the currency in the first place. Currencies can fluctuate enormously in a short period of time, but they tend to trend in one direction or another unless the economic factor propelling them is changed. However, interventions often cause significant currency movement in a short period of time, so they are enormous opportunities for traders. If a central bank defends its currency, causing it to lurch in one direction, traders can bet that it will eventually resume its course.

Another way to look at interventions is that they are a sign that something in the world economy is out of balance. By the end of the 1980s, Japanese exports had made sizeable inroads in the U.S.

economy, partly because the yen traded low against the U.S. dollar, making Japanese imports to the U.S. cheaper than domestic competition. The Japanese government wanted to keep this balance in its favor. By the end of the 1980s, the dollar was again rising, and the Fed decided to intervene to force the dollar lower. Between April 29 and October 12, 1989, it spent more than $10 billion to lower the dollar. The intervention, however, did little. The dollar began to fall only when the Japanese had accumulated so many dollars that they were forced to put them back into circulation. The yen finally rose, and Japanese companies used it to buy American assets.

Scams and Rogue Traders

For a short time in the mid-1990s, Forex became the dumping ground for failed equity brokers and scam artists. Individuals who were either suspended from trading stocks or could never get their series 7 quietly moved to Forex. It provided the ideal market. It was shrouded in myth, had high volatility, and was unregulated. In addition, brokers could easily ask for trading discretion (because the market was open 24 hours) and through high frequency trading generate huge commissions. Whereas in stocks they would have to make a new sale every time to generate revenue. The fundamental way to trade Forex is to move quickly in and out of trades, each time generating a commission for the broker (either as a straight commission or as part of the spread). What was considered churing in the stock market was normal trading in Forex. This means that $100,000 can become a money-generating machine with no regulatory protection afforded to the investor.

Although there have been a few spectacular scams, few are as sophisticated and dramatic as Evergreen International and First Equity (bogus clearing firms). If it had not been for the World

Trade Center collapse, this sham might still be going on. According to the charges, two executives and three companies were engaged in mail and wire fraud, conspiracy, and money laundering that resulted in the loss of $100 million by about 1,400 investors in Australia, New Zealand, the U.S., and Europe.

The scam started in 1997, when Evergreen used cold-calling techniques perfected in the boiler rooms of the 1990s bull market to solicit money from all over the world. This scam really had nothing to do with Forex except for the fact that Forex provided the perfect vehicle. No Forex trades were actually ever made. The lure of Forex trading is easy to realize—it has global appeal but is poorly understood. It had the fantasy of easy, no-risk profits and was inaccessible to smaller investors.

According to U.S. authorities, investors would deposit funds in the First Equity bank account in Australia, New Zealand, or New York with the intention of becoming part of a managed account (which promised over 24 percent annual returns). First Equity was actually owned by Evergreen, although clients were told it was a separate entity. After the money was deposited—and without the client's knowledge—it was transferred through a complex series of accounts. It ended up in a Budapest bank account, or it was just blatantly withdrawn to fund employee extravagance. Evergreen had offices in the Trump building on Wall Street, in the World Trade Center, and on Park Avenue South. These were very upscale locations selected to impress investors and employees.

For a while, it worked. Investors were sent fake monthly statements showing sizeable increases to their accounts, while brokers continued to call and sign up more victims. If a client wanted to withdraw a fund, he was pressured to stay in. If he was unyielding, Evergreen simply used funds from a new client.

The U.S. Attorney for the Eastern District of New York, Alan Vinegrad, later described the scheme: "The defendants solicited money through a series of lies, misused these funds for their own personal use and to line the pockets of their employees and falsely assured the investors that their money was available to them, when in fact it was transferred from company to company until it was beyond their reach."

On September 11, 2001, the collapse of the World Trade Center towers destroyed First Equity. The owner, Andre Kouachev, realized that his scam would come under the scrutiny of insurers, government investigators, and investors. He fled the country, and the FBI is still looking for him. When all was said and done, only $1 million of the $100 million was ever recovered.

The Evergreen scam is only one of many similar stories. Currency trading can offer such fantastic returns in short periods of time that even investors who should know better get caught up in the hype and burned in scams.

One of the most famous occurred in Princeton, New Jersey, where Charles Kohli managed $60 million in currency speculation. Although Kohli had experienced success in the 1980s and early 1990s, his formulas and predictions began to go wrong. Either he was unable to adjust to changes in the market or he made some bad decisions, but in any case he was soon losing millions. Rather than pass on this information to investors, Kohli covered it up. He reported dazzling gains with fictitious statements and opened attractive offices to win more investors. For a time, it worked. But Kohli kept losing money, and in the end his empire collapsed. Investors lost $40 million, and Kohli was sent to prison for fraud.

Many times, fraud and scams occur not between unsuspecting individuals and institutions, but within the institutions themselves.

Consider the case of Barings Bank, one of Britain's oldest and most prestigious financial institutions. It had helped finance the Napoleonic wars, the Louisiana Purchase, and the Erie Canal. It had prospered for centuries.

Then along came Nick Leeson, who grew up in London and joined Barings after graduating from university. He applied for and was given a transfer to the Far East. Before long, he was trading for Barings Securities Limited in Singapore (BSS). Through a fatal oversight, Leeson was promoted to being both the manager and the head trader at BSS. In effect, he was boss of himself, with no one looking over his shoulder.

From his tiny office in Singapore, Leeson began taking unauthorized, speculative positions. It appears that he lost money from the beginning. When losses mounted, he hid them in a special account numbered 88888. At the end of 1992, the account held 2 million pounds. At the end of 1993, it had reached 23 million pounds. A year later, it had jumped to 208 million pounds.

Leeson might still have emerged unscathed and made good on his losses, but then a massive earthquake struck Kobe, an industrialized area in Japan. It took a few days before investors realized the extent of the devastation, but by then the nikkei had dropped like a stone. Leeson, who had bet heavily on a rising Japanese stock market, saw his losses balloon to 827 million pounds.

Leeson had used his position to draw lines of credit and conceal his activities from Barings. Once the world learned what had happened, Barings Bank collapsed.

Leeson, in the meantime, tried to flee to England. He was arrested in Frankfurt and returned to Singapore, where he was sentenced to six-and-a-half years in prison for fraud. He wrote an account of his dealings entitled Rogue Trader, which was published in 1996. Three years later, he was released from prison with time off for good behavior.

One of the lessons of Leeson's story is that no trader, no matter how good or how prepared, can anticipate everything. Leeson, it turned out, had taken a very sensible position, betting that Japan's economy would grow. So had many other traders, but the earthquake made those strategies useless.

The other lesson from the collapse of Barings was that banks needed to improve their internal controls—but not every bank learned the lesson. Over several years, starting in 1997, a trader named John Rusnak for Allfirst Bank in Baltimore began taking aggressive positions on the yen/dollar. By 2000, Rusnak positions had yielded a loss of $690 million. Like Leeson, Rusnak concealed his losses while reporting profits, which in turn won him and his staff record bonuses. In 2003, Rusnak was sentenced to more than seven years in prison for fraud.

Russia Devalues the Ruble

An investor should understand that government can sometimes make decisions that are as unpredictable and stunning as an earthquake.

In 1998, the Russian government faced a growing crisis. The nation's banking system was still primitive nearly eight years after the fall of the Soviet Union. Investors were unsure about the stability of the ruble, and pressure began to build as they traded in rubles for dollars.

Officially, the government defended the exchange rate. In July, an international bailout committed $22 billion in new loans for the Russian government. Everything, it seemed, would work out. On Friday, August 14, President Boris Yeltsin publicly vowed that the ruble would not be devalued.

On Monday, August 17, the government and Russian central bank announced that the ruble would be devalued 50 percent by the end of 1998 and that trading was suspended in government bonds. The announcement was a shock to the markets. The Russian central bank was forced to spend $1 billion in the following weeks just to ensure that the ruble didn't fall too far too fast.

How do you incorporate the unknown into your trading strategy? Be sure to include a special plan in case something does occur that changes everything. Have it ready, and rehearse in your mind exactly what you will do if that "X factor," or black swan, appears.

12

TRENDS AND THE YUAN

Forex typically makes any so-called "trend spotter" appear foolish. While I was writing and editing this chapter, Southeast Asia changed forever. An undersea earthquake caused giant waves to slam into coastlines throughout the region. In just a few horrifying minutes, hundreds of thousands of people were killed. Outside of the human cost, governments and economies were forced to adjust in a matter of days. This is a perfect example of chaos theory and the interconnectivity of today's global markets. No analyst, of course, predicted this "X factor" or Black Swan in his daily reports. But it has dominated the market psyche, and it has forever altered the region.

The larger lesson is that this market is too dynamic to pin down. However, this chapter discusses some trends and issues I see coming up in Forex's future—things to keep your eyes open for.

Forex Will Not Just Get Bigger; It Will Get More Respect

In September 2004, the *Wall Street Journal* declared that "Foreign Exchange has now shown itself to be a viable asset class." Like many other analysts and market watchers, I am confident that Forex will attract more investors because of the unique market conditions it offers. I also believe, however, that industry regulators will make the market a safer and more predictable place to invest, and that investors will respond. This confidence and opportunity will not be lost on American investors, who have tended to be less aware of the importance of currencies due to the supremacy of the U.S. dollar. I expect American investors will start routinely putting some of their money in the Forex markets and that they will begin to scan the international news and currency columns more carefully, as their counterparts in Asia and Europe have done for decades. Get ready to start hearing about currency cross rates around the water cooler.

Globalization and the War on Terror

With all the benefits of globalization and living in an interconnected world, there are some significant downsides. One of these is terrorism. Regardless of the U.S.'s "war on terror," terrorism is here to stay. Antisocial groups have recognized the enormous power of terrorist acts. Although terrorism itself is not a new development in history, terrorists' ability to strike around the world and with enormous destructive power is. Typically, terrorists have been isolated to a disputed region; today, they realize the effectiveness of attacking abroad. For traders, this raises two concerns.

One is the scope of the attacks, because even the destruction of nonfinancial targets can have profound effects on a country's economy, as witnessed in the U.S. and Spain. If an attack occurs, Forex will be the first market to react. The speed, volatility, and unpredictability of this crime make it a major factor in future currency trading.

The second concern is that terrorists might target the financial system itself. Although there is no proof that any single entity is moving currency around to damage a nation, there has been ample speculation, especially after September 11. There were rumors that a few days before the attacks, some unusually large positions against the U.S. dollar were taken in Europe by unknown entities. While I haven't reviewed the issue with any experts (although some very smart traders have said the trades are on the books), it raises a serious issue. Given enough capital and trading access, and given the right market conditions, someone could do serious damage to the world financial markets. In an attempt to limit this activity, and to try to immobilize assets in accounts, Congress has passed an anti-money-laundering policy in the Patriot Act. It has been somewhat effective in the U.S., but it has very little influence outside U.S. borders, and this is a global marketplace.

I'm not predicting whether the "war on terror" will end in an American victory, and I have no idea whether Iraq will become a stable democracy or collapse into violence. Terrorism, however, is here to stay.

The Chinese Dragon and the Indian Tiger

If you've read any major Western newspaper or magazine, you've probably seen a feature on China and the enormous economic potential that nation represents. *BusinessWeek* called it "the world's second-most important economy."

From 1984 to 2004, China logged an average annual GDP growth of 10 percent. (The average rate of growth in developed countries has been about 3 percent.) From 1993 to 2004, exports grew on average 17 percent annually. Today China trails only the U.S., Japan, and Germany in total export volume. In 2003, China for the first time took in more foreign direct investment than the U.S.

In November 2004, *BusinessWeek* reporter David Cohen wrote that China's "policy moves are being watched and weighed as never before. With China increasingly seen as a vital engine for world growth, markets have begun to treat its economic data and policy moves much as they would those of any other global economic powerhouse."

One of the most interesting stories in foreign exchange today is what will happen to China's currency, the yuan. At the time this chapter was written, the yuan was pegged to the U.S. dollar. Today, 7.28 yuan buys $1. The success of this policy has been twofold. First, it has provided the country with the stability it needs for economic growth. Second, it has held down costs and given China's goods a competitive edge.

China has become a gateway for Asian goods to enter the world markets. Its manufacturing base pulls in components from all over eastern Asia, assembles them, and exports them—especially to the U.S. And that's become a problem. The U.S. trade deficit with China has soared to $150 billion.

As the Chinese-American trade balance has swung sharply off balance, global pressure has been mounting on the Chinese government to allow its currency to float—that is, trade at its market value. From a currency trader's perspective, this peg makes China one of the most intriguing puzzles in the world.

The peg, say many, cannot last. It leads to massive global imbalances as China's goods, artificially cheap, flood world markets. The U.S. dollar must decline in value to restore a realistic balance to the U.S.-China trade relationship. The flow of U.S. dollars into China has swollen China's foreign exchange reserves to $514.5 billion, second only to Japan. In Europe, officials mutter that China's peg has allowed other East Asian nations to maintain their own pegs to the U.S. dollar, thus magnifying the effect of the trade imbalance. Unfortunately for European manufacturers, the decline in the U.S. dollar has been borne primarily by the euro. Consequently, officials from around the world have been insistently calling for China to end its peg to the U.S. dollar and allow the yuan to float.

Some China watchers insist that the Chinese government will not do anything so quick or drastic. The current exchange rate benefits China's exporters and allows them to provide more employment and repay their loans to state-run banks. China's government would not willingly damage its position.

Rather, the government may allow the currency to gradually expand its trading range and thus drift up to its natural value over time. The Chinese government has made some statements that appear to suggest that such a strategy is under consideration.

"Don't expect anything more than baby steps on currency reform," wrote reporter Dexter Roberts in *BusinessWeek*. "The betting is that Beijing will do just enough to quell its critics abroad—but not enough to jeopardize growth prospects at home." (*BusinessWeek*, March 8, 2004, Issue 3873, p. 31, 1p, 1c) This would be the best way for a foreign exchange trader to view the market, but watch out when the peg gets loosened.

Roberts said many analysts believe the yuan is undervalued by 20 to 40 percent. Currently, China has maintained its relationship with the U.S. by pouring its surplus money back into U.S. securities, mostly treasuries. For a long time, this has kept yields low and the dollar higher. If the Chinese abandon that strategy (and there is disagreement among economists about whether this will happen), the dollar would almost certainly decline in value.

According to the *Economist,* Asian central banks are "subsidizing rather than punishing American profligacy, allowing deficits to grow for longer. When the inevitable correction comes, it will be all the more painful."

The *Economist* also argues that allowing the yuan to float would not necessarily mean the currency would rise higher. Chinese households would diversify many of their assets by exchanging yuan for foreign currencies, thus keeping the currency low. "Overall, therefore, the case for a big yuan revaluation is weaker than is commonly claimed," the magazine concluded. ("A fair exchange?", the *Economist,* Oct. 2, 2004, Vol. 372, Issue 8395, special section p. 14, 3p, 1 graph, 1c)

Foreign exchange participants will be asking the following questions: How stable is the yuan? How much risk is attached to holding it? Is the yuan a viable currency to hold in the short and long term? If there is inherent risk in holding the yuan, it will stay an untradeable currency, and people who need yuan for business transactions will find alternative ways to transact commerce. They will probably use another currency for most transactions and hold a small amount of yuan for short periods.

From a trader's perspective, knowing the exact outcome is less important than having a prepared response and a willingness to act. In any case, the ability to trade the yuan will add another currency to the marketplace, where a savvy trader can find opportunities. I believe the prospect of trading the remimbi (yuan) to be very exciting, whether it is opened to trading by government policy or by the force of the market. There will be some extraordinary opportunities.

The source of some of these opportunities will be because China's economic success is by no means a sure thing. China, after all, faces enormous challenges, and any economic shock could change all assumptions. Population growth, weakness in the banking sector, significant social change, and a rigid political system are major hurdles.

Considering all these factors, Chinese officials can be forgiven if they get little sleep at night. Currency traders, on the other hand, should see all these factors for what they are—possible sources of currency movement. Or, in another word, opportunity. Will China's officials make the right decisions about these problems? Those answers could well move China's currency.

China, however, may not be the biggest story in Asia. In fact, it may not even be the most populous country. That distinction could well go to India, which is forecast to surpass China's population by 2030. This is not the only reason to pay attention to India; it also could become the next great economic powerhouse.

India, like China, has been undergoing dramatic economic changes. Since the 1990s, it has turned away from the state-run economic policies that long stifled economic growth. Due to the legacy of the British Empire, it has a reservoir of highly educated English speakers (that's why all those call centers have been outsourced to India). It also has a thriving Internet technology industry, and its workers are far cheaper to pay than those in the U.S. Moreover, India is a functioning democracy (the largest in the world) and is committed to economic growth as a way to pull its hundreds of millions of citizens out of poverty.

India's infrastructure, however, is still substandard, and its manufacturing base doesn't get nearly as much attention as China's. But this could be changing. Major companies—including Toyota—are moving factories to India for export to other Southeast Asian markets. As the country grows economically, hundreds of millions may enter the middle class, making it the second-largest potential new market behind China.

Unlike the yuan, India's currency, the rupee, is widely traded outside the U.S. It is likely to fluctuate with the country's fortunes. As with China, this offers traders opportunities.

ASEAN

The Association of Southeast Asian Nations (ASEAN) was established on August 8, 1967 in Bangkok by five nations: Indonesia, Malaysia, the Philippines, Singapore, and Thailand. Brunei Darussalam joined in 1984, Vietnam in 1995, Laos and Myanmar in 1997, and Cambodia in 1999. The population of ASEAN is about 500 million, and it has a combined GDP of almost $750 billion.

The growing power of the Southeastern Asian economies has inspired an unlikely idea—a common currency for the entire region. The *Economist* once asked ASEAN's chairman when a common currency might actually come about. He turned and pointed to the youngest person in the room. "Perhaps in her lifetime," he answered.

A common currency—following the same blueprint of the EMU—would change the world. The economies of South Korea, China, and Japan, along with those of the smaller nations, would form an economic powerhouse on par with the U.S. and Europe. The project would also unite under one economy peoples who have warred for centuries and possibly create a united political system, duplicating a process achieved in Europe.

The instruments of this unification would probably be similar. It would start with baby steps, perhaps an agreement on a commodity or a small pact between just a few core countries. As the system took hold and prospered, however, it would attract new members and deeper commitments.

The Euro: Can It Hold?

Since its physical launch in 2002 (although it was available electronically for years before that), the euro has emerged as a powerful counterweight to the U.S. dollar. As many of its architects hoped, it is unseating the U.S. dollar's supremacy in world currency markets. The U.S. dollar suffered larger reverses against the euro in 2004. If central banks outside the U.S. begin exchanging their reserves of dollars for euros, the U.S. dollar may experience an even more drastic decline.

The euro, however, will face enormous pressures over the long run that may lead to its undoing. This is a complicated scenario, but here are some possible outcomes.

The first outcome, of course, is that the euro may replace the dollar as the world's reserve currency. In this scenario, the European economies, liberated by crushing regulation, finally expand and grow again. With healthy economies and a strong currency, Europe successfully integrates new members in the east (including Turkey), funds its generous welfare system, and creates jobs. The U.S., with its failing education system, declining currency, and costly military entanglements abroad, falls steadily behind. This is the scenario euro planners dream about.

On the opposite end of the spectrum is the pessimistic scenario. The European Union (EU) expands and becomes unwieldy with so many members. Western Europe's birthrates fall to catastrophic lows, and "Old Europe" steadily loses population. With fewer workers, Europe can't fund its welfare systems, and the societies become divided between old and young. Desperate for labor, Europe attracts millions of Muslim immigrants from the Middle East and North Africa. These immigrants can't or won't assimilate, and European society experiences destabilizing shocks. Under these pressures, the European Union dissolves, and the euro collapses. These two scenarios are extreme, but they represent the broader issues facing the euro.

Short-term threats also exist. The European Union has borders that are potentially destabilizing, unlike the U.S., which is buffered by two oceans. Russia, which could become hostile, lies to the east. The Balkans, where genocidal civil war raged just a decade ago, are to the southeast. North Africa is across the Mediterranean Sea. If the EU expansion includes Turkey, the EU will have a border on the Middle East. Trouble in any of these areas may not directly threaten the EU, but it might force the EU to spend more money on aid and the military. If the trouble becomes serious and the U.S. becomes more isolationist after the Iraq war, the EU might have to devote enormous funds to secure stability. In any case, this is unlikely to help the currency.

The Growth of Free-Trade Blocks

The success of NAFTA and the Eurozone has many policy makers believing in the virtues of free trade. Currently, there are serious discussions of a free-trade western hemisphere, as well as the creation of free-trade zones in Southeast Asia. Whether these individual initiatives fail or succeed is irrelevant. The longer-term trend is toward more free trade, and this will create more opportunities for Forex traders.

The U.S. Dollar

Since the end of World War II, the U.S. dollar has been the bedrock of global growth. It has been treated literally like gold—as something so dependable that banks and nations can hold it in reserve. The role of the dollar has been one of the reasons the U.S. has been able to achieve its preeminent position in the world today.

Is that about to change?

Since 2002, the U.S. dollar has been in trouble. It has slipped dramatically against most major currencies, especially the euro. The U.S. trade account deficit has hit 5.7 percent of the U.S. GDP, a historic high that economists agree is unsustainable. The U.S. needs an average of $1.8 billion of foreign capital every day to sustain it, sucking in most of the world's savings in the process. Along with the current account deficit, the U.S. government spends more than it takes in. These twin deficits, say critics, doom the dollar to a dramatic devaluation that could have a disastrous effect on the global economy. Moreover, unlike in the past, the euro has emerged as an alternative to the dollar. If foreigners lose confidence in the U.S. or refuse to loan it more money, they might convert their assets to the euro.

This would be especially devastating to the U.S. economy. In effect, the U.S. has enjoyed the ability to pay its bills (including oil) in its own currency. Theoretically, if bills to foreign creditors rise, the U.S. can simply print more money to pay them. If the dollar loses its current position as the world's reserve currency, this privilege will be gone. The U.S. will have to live within its means like other nations, leading to a drop in consumer spending and a recession—possibly a depression.

For a trader, the question to ask is how the U.S. government and society react to the trade and federal deficits. If Congress and the White House continue to spend like there is no tomorrow, expect the currency markets to take notice. If American consumers also consume without thought of saving, the trade deficit will only worsen, and the dollar's value will fall with it. Although no one can predict what will happen, the global imbalances that exist today must be resolved—and they will be. On the one hand, you can never count the U.S. out. It has an enormously successful economy, a society with an entrepreneurial culture, a history of assimilating talented immigrants, and a democratic system that has survived more than 200 years. It is also protected by two oceans and is at peace with its neighbors. On the other hand, these imbalances are at historic levels, and the U.S. dollar may be punished because of it. As always, these imbalances represent an opportunity. Every trader must be prepared for what happens and be ready to act.

Endnotes

1. *BusinessWeek,* Nov. 9, 2004, www.businessweek.com/bwdaily/dnflash/nov2004/nf2004119_0024_PG2_db039.htm.

APPENDIX

CURRENCY LIST

AFA	Afghanistan, Afghanis
ALL	Albania, Leke
DZD	Algeria, Dinars
USD	America (United States of America), Dollars
USD	American Samoa, United States Dollars
USD	American Virgin Islands, United States Dollars
EUR	Andorra, Euro
AOA	Angola, Kwanza
XCD	Anguilla, East Caribbean Dollars

XCD	Antigua and Barbuda, East Caribbean Dollars
ARS	Argentina, Pesos
AMD	Armenia, Drams
AWG	Aruba, Guilders (also called Florins)
ANG	Aruba, Netherlands Antilles Guilders (also called Florins)
AUD	Australia, Dollars
EUR	Austria, Euro
AZM	Azerbaijan, Manats
EUR	Azores, Euro
BSD	Bahamas, Dollars
BHD	Bahrain, Dinars
EUR	Baleares (Balearic Islands), Euro
BDT	Bangladesh, Taka
BBD	Barbados, Dollars
XCD	Barbuda and Antigua, East Caribbean Dollars
BYR	Belarus, Rubles
EUR	Belgium, Euro
BZD	Belize, Dollars
XOF	Benin, Communauté Financière Africaine Francs (BCEAO)
BMD	Bermuda, Dollars
BTN	Bhutan, Ngultrum
INR	Bhutan, India Rupeess
BOB	Bolivia, Bolivianos
ANG	Bonaire, Netherlands Antilles Guilders (also called Florins)

BAM	Bosnia and Herzegovina, Convertible Marka
BWP	Botswana, Pulas
NOK	Bouvet Island, Norway Kroner
BRL	Brazil, Real
GBP	Britain (United Kingdom), Pounds
USD	British Indian Ocean Territory, United States Dollars
USD	British Virgin Islands, United States Dollars
BND	Brunei Darussalam, Dollars
BGN	Bulgaria, Leva
XOF	Burkina Faso, Communauté Financière Africaine Francs (BCEAO)
MMK	Burma (Myanmar), Kyats
BIF	Burundi, Francs
XOF	Côte D'Ivoire, Communauté Financière Africaine Francs (BCEAO)
USD	Caicos and Turks Islands, United States Dollars
KHR	Cambodia, Riels
XAF	Cameroon, Communauté Financière Africaine Francs (BEAC)
CAD	Canada, Dollars
EUR	Canary Islands, Euro
CVE	Cape Verde, Escudos
KYD	Cayman Islands, Dollars
XAF	Central African Republic, Communauté Financière Africaine Francs (BEAC)
XAF	Chad, Communauté Financière Africaine Francs (BEAC)

CLP	Chile, Pesos
CNY	China, Yuan Renminbi
AUD	Christmas Island, Australia Dollars
AUD	Cocos (Keeling) Islands, Australia Dollars
COP	Colombia, Pesos
XAF	Communauté Financière Africaine (CFA), Francs
KMF	Comoros, Francs
XPF	Comptoirs Français du Pacifique (CFP), Francs
XAF	Congo/Brazzaville, Communauté Financière Africaine Francs (BEAC)
CDF	Congo/Kinshasa, Francs
NZD	Cook Islands, New Zealand Dollars
CRC	Costa Rica, Colones
HRK	Croatia, Kuna
CUP	Cuba, Pesos
ANG	Curaço, Netherlands Antilles Guilders (also called Florins)
CYP	Cyprus, Pounds
CZK	Czech Republic, Koruny
DKK	Denmark, Kroner
DJF	Djibouti, Francs
XCD	Dominica, East Caribbean Dollars
DOP	Dominican Republic, Pesos
EUR	Dutch (Netherlands) Euro
XCD	East Caribbean Dollars
IDR	East Timor, Indonesia Rupiahs
USD	Ecuador, United States Dollars

EGP	Egypt, Pounds
EUR	Eire (Ireland), Euro
SVC	El Salvador, Colones
GBP	England (United Kingdom), Pounds
XAF	Equatorial Guinea, Communauté Financière Africaine Francs (BEAC)
ETB	Eritrea, Ethiopia Birr
ERN	Eritrea, Nakfa
EEK	Estonia, Krooni
ETB	Ethiopia, Birr
EUR	Euro Member Countries, Euro
FKP	Falkland Islands (Malvinas), Pounds
DKK	Faroe Islands, Denmark Kroner
FJD	Fiji, Dollars
EUR	Finland, Euro
EUR	France, Euro
EUR	French Guiana, Euro
XPF	French Pacific Islands (French Polynesia), Comptoirs Français du Pacifique Francs
XPF	French Polynesia (French Pacific Islands), Comptoirs Français du Pacifique Francs
EUR	French Southern Territories, Euro
XPF	Futuna and Wallis Islands, Comptoirs Français du Pacifique Francs
XAF	Gabon, Communauté Financière Africaine Francs (BEAC)
GMD	Gambia, Dalasi

GEL	Georgia, Lari
EUR	Germany, Euro
GHC	Ghana, Cedis
GIP	Gibraltar, Pounds
XAU	Gold, Ounces
GBP	Great Britain (United Kingdom), Pounds
EUR	Greece, Euro
DKK	Greenland, Denmark Kroner
XCD	Grenada, East Caribbean Dollars
XCD	Grenadines (The) and Saint Vincent, East Caribbean Dollars
EUR	Guadeloupe, Euro
USD	Guam, United States Dollars
GTQ	Guatemala, Quetzales
GGP	Guernsey, Pounds
GNF	Guinea, Francs
XOF	Guinea-Bissau, Communauté Financière Africaine Francs (BCEAO)
GYD	Guyana, Dollars
HTG	Haiti, Gourdes
USD	Haiti, United States Dollars
AUD	Heard Island and McDonald Islands, Australia Dollars
BAM	Herzegovina and Bosnia, Convertible Marka
EUR	Holland (Netherlands), Euro
EUR	Holy See, (Vatican City), Euro
HNL	Honduras, Lempiras

HKD	Hong Kong, Dollars
HUF	Hungary, Forint
ISK	Iceland, Kronur
INR	India, Rupees
IDR	Indonesia, Rupiahs
XDR	International Monetary Fund (IMF), Special Drawing Rights
IRR	Iran, Rials
IQD	Iraq, Dinars
EUR	Ireland (Eire), Euro
IMP	Isle of Man, Pounds
ILS	Israel, New Shekels
EUR	Italy, Euro
JMD	Jamaica, Dollars
NOK	Jan Mayen and Svalbard, Norway Kroner
JPY	Japan, Yen
JEP	Jersey, Pounds
JOD	Jordan, Dinars
KZT	Kazakhstan, Tenge
AUD	Keeling (Cocos) Islands, Australia Dollars
KES	Kenya, Shillings
AUD	Kiribati, Australia Dollars
KPW	Korea (North), Won
KRW	Korea (South), Won
KWD	Kuwait, Dinars
KGS	Kyrgyzstan, Soms

LAK	Laos, Kips
LVL	Latvia, Lati
LBP	Lebanon, Pounds
LSL	Lesotho, Maloti
ZAR	Lesotho, South Africa Rand
LRD	Liberia, Dollars
LYD	Libya, Dinars
CHF	Liechtenstein, Switzerland Francs
LTL	Lithuania, Litai
EUR	Luxembourg, Euro
MOP	Macau, Patacas
MKD	Macedonia, Denars
MGA	Madagascar, Ariary
EUR	Madeira Islands, Euro
MWK	Malawi, Kwachas
MYR	Malaysia, Ringgits
MVR	Maldives (Maldive Islands), Rufiyaa
XOF	Mali, Communauté Financière Africaine Francs (BCEAO)
MTL	Malta, Liri
FKP	Malvinas (Falkland Islands), Pounds
USD	Mariana Islands (Northern), United States Dollars
USD	Marshall Islands, United States Dollars
EUR	Martinique, Euro
MRO	Mauritania, Ouguiyas
MUR	Mauritius, Rupees
EUR	Mayotte, Euro

AUD	McDonald Islands and Heard Island, Australia Dollars
MXN	Mexico, Pesos
USD	Micronesia (Federated States of), United States Dollars
USD	Midway Islands, United States Dollars
EUR	Miquelon and Saint Pierre, Euro
MDL	Moldova, Lei
EUR	Monaco, Euro
MNT	Mongolia, Tugriks
EUR	Montenegro, Euro
XCD	Montserrat, East Caribbean Dollars
MAD	Morocco, Dirhams
MZM	Mozambique, Meticais
MMK	Myanmar (Burma), Kyats
NAD	Namibia, Dollars
ZAR	Namibia, South Africa Rand
AUD	Nauru, Australia Dollars
NPR	Nepal, Rupees
ANG	Netherlands Antilles, Guilders (also called Florins)
EUR	Netherlands, Euro
XCD	Nevis and Saint Kitts, East Caribbean Dollars
XPF	New Caledonia, Comptoirs Français du Pacifique Francs
NZD	New Zealand, Dollars
NIO	Nicaragua, Cordobas
XOF	Niger, Communauté Financière Africaine Francs (BCEAO)

NGN	Nigeria, Nairas
NZD	Niue, New Zealand Dollars
AUD	Norfolk Island, Australia Dollars
USD	Northern Mariana Islands, United States Dollars
NOK	Norway, Kroner
OMR	Oman, Rials
PKR	Pakistan, Rupees
USD	Palau, United States Dollars
XPD	Palladium, Ounces
PAB	Panama, Balboa
USD	Panama, United States Dollars
PGK	Papua New Guinea, Kina
PYG	Paraguay, Guarani
PEN	Peru, Nuevos Soles
PHP	Philippines, Pesos
NZD	Pitcairn Islands, New Zealand Dollars
XPT	Platinum, Ounces
PLN	Poland, Zlotych
EUR	Portugal, Euro
STD	Principe and São Tome, Dobras
USD	Puerto Rico, United States Dollars
QAR	Qatar, Rials
EUR	Réunion, Euro
ROL	Romania, Lei
RUB	Russia, Rubles
RWF	Rwanda, Francs
STD	São Tome and Principe, Dobras

ANG	Saba, Netherlands Antilles Guilders (also called Florins)
MAD	Sahara (Western), Morocco Dirhams
XCD	Saint Christopher, East Caribbean Dollars
SHP	Saint Helena, Pounds
XCD	Saint Kitts and Nevis, East Caribbean Dollars
XCD	Saint Lucia, East Caribbean Dollars
EUR	Saint Pierre and Miquelon, Euro
XCD	Saint Vincent and The Grenadines, East Caribbean Dollars
EUR	Saint-Martin, Euro
USD	Samoa (American), United States Dollars
WST	Samoa, Tala
EUR	San Marino, Euro
SAR	Saudi Arabia, Riyals
SPL	Seborga, Luigini
XOF	Senegal, Communauté Financière Africaine Francs (BCEAO)
CSD	Serbia, Dinars
SCR	Seychelles, Rupees
SLL	Sierra Leone, Leones
XAG	Silver, Ounces
SGD	Singapore, Dollars
ANG	Sint Eustatius, Netherlands Antilles Guilders (also called Florins)
ANG	Sint Maarten, Netherlands Antilles Guilders (also called Florins)

SKK	Slovakia, Koruny
SIT	Slovenia, Tolars
SBD	Solomon Islands, Dollars
SOS	Somalia, Shillings
ZAR	South Africa, Rand
GBP	South Georgia, United Kingdom Pounds
GBP	South Sandwich Islands, United Kingdom Pounds
EUR	Spain, Euro
XDR	Special Drawing Rights
LKR	Sri Lanka, Rupees
SDD	Sudan, Dinars
SRD	Suriname, Dollars
NOK	Svalbard and Jan Mayen, Norway Kroner
SZL	Swaziland, Emalangeni
SEK	Sweden, Kronor
CHF	Switzerland, Francs
SYP	Syria, Pounds
TWD	Taiwan, New Dollars
RUB	Tajikistan, Russia Rubles
TJS	Tajikistan, Somoni
TZS	Tanzania, Shillings
THB	Thailand, Baht
IDR	Timor (East), Indonesia Rupiahs
TTD	Tobago and Trinidad, Dollars
XOF	Togo, Communauté Financière Africaine Francs (BCEAO)
NZD	Tokelau, New Zealand Dollars

TOP	Tonga, Pa'anga
TTD	Trinidad and Tobago, Dollars
TND	Tunisia, Dinars
TRL	Turkey, Liras [being phased out]
TRY	Turkey, New Lira
TMM	Turkmenistan, Manats
USD	Turks and Caicos Islands, United States Dollars
TVD	Tuvalu, Tuvalu Dollars
UGX	Uganda, Shillings
UAH	Ukraine, Hryvnia
AED	United Arab Emirates, Dirhams
GBP	United Kingdom, Pounds
USD	United States Minor Outlying Islands, United States Dollars
USD	United States of America, Dollars
UYU	Uruguay, Pesos
USD	US Virgin Islands, United States Dollars
UZS	Uzbekistan, Sums
VUV	Vanuatu, Vatu
EUR	Vatican City (The Holy See), Euro
VEB	Venezuela, Bolivares
VND	Viet Nam, Dong
USD	Virgin Islands (American), United States Dollars
USD	Virgin Islands (British), United States Dollars
USD	Wake Island, United States Dollars
XPF	Wallis and Futuna Islands, Comptoirs Français du Pacifique Francs

WST	West Samoa (Samoa), Tala
MAD	Western Sahara, Morocco Dirhams
WST	Western Samoa (Samoa), Tala
YER	Yemen, Rials
ZMK	Zambia, Kwacha
ZWD	Zimbabwe, Zimbabwe Dollars

INDEX

Reference critical business skills in an instant online.

Try it **FREE!**
Sign up for a 30-day Enterprise Trial at
www.safaribooksonline.com/bizdemo.asp

SEARCH electronic versions of hundreds of books simultaneously.

BROWSE books by category. Peruse the latest titles from today's most authoritative business authors.

FIND answers in an instant!

Search Safari! Zero in on exactly the information you need to complete the task at hand - from creating killer presentations, to understanding how supply chains work, to honing your interview skills. Search across all books in the library simultaneously to pinpoint exactly the chapter, sentence and example you need. Read books from cover to cover. Or, flip right to the page you need.

Safari®
BUSINESS BOOKS ONLINE

Preview Safari as our guest at bus.safaribooksonline.com or sign up for a free enterprise trial at www.safaribooksonline.com/bizdemo.asp. Also check out Safari's premier library for programmers and IT professionals at safari.informit.com.

Options Trading for the Conservative Investor
Increasing Profits Without Increasing Your Risk
BY MICHAEL C. THOMSETT

Options don't have to be high-risk, complicated, or exotic: in fact, they're a powerful tool for conservative stock investors aiming to limit risk. In *Options Trading for the Conservative Investor*, Michael C. Thomsett demonstrates how carefully chosen options strategies can help investors consistently improve their returns without taking on unacceptable risk. Thomsett—author of the global best-seller *Getting Started in Options*—writes in simple, non-technical language, uses real examples, and guides you through every strategy, one easy step at a time. He's made this book simple and visual enough for any stock investor to use—even if they have no previous experience trading options.

ISBN 0131497855, © 2005, 288 pp., $34.95

Technical Analysis
Power Tools for Active Investors
BY GERALD APPEL

In this book, one of the world's most respected technical analysts offers a complete course in forecasting future market behavior through cyclical, trend, momentum, and volume signals. What's more, unlike most books on this subject, Gerald Appel's *Technical Analysis* offers step-by-step instructions virtually any investor can use to achieve breakthrough success in the market. Appel illuminates a wide range of strategies and timing models, demystifying even advanced technical analysis the first time. Among the models he covers: NASDAQ/NYSE Relative Strength, 3-5 Year Treasury Notes, Triple Momentum, Seasonality, Breadth-Thrust Impulse, and models based on the revolutionary MACD techniques he personally invented.

ISBN 0131479024, © 2005, 264 pp., $44.95